North American

Marsh Birds

North American

Marsh Birds

Gary Low

William Mansell

1817

HARPER & ROW, PUBLISHERS, New York

Cambridge, Philadelphia, San Francisco, London
Mexico City, São Paulo, Sydney

FIRST EDITION

LIBRARY OF CONGRESS CATALOG CARD NUMBER: 83-479-15
ISBN 0-06-015216-8

To our wives,
who suffered as much in this production
as did we.

Contents

Foreword

When Gary Low suggested that this, our second book, be on marsh birds, I readily concurred, seeing in it an opportunity to crusade for the preservation of marshes and their inhabitants. It was not to be a Doomsday Book in the tenor of the many articles that have appeared on the same subject, nor an approach so light-hearted it would defeat our purpose, but one that would follow a path well inside the extremes. We hope I have not strayed far from that course and that the presentation of the lives of some of our marsh birds, so delicately painted and drawn by Gary, will arouse your interest in them and therefore in the conservation of their homes. If I succeed in saving one marsh, I shall feel amply repaid.

There is little to explain about the format. The ranges of the species are given broadly, just as their food is generalized. The numbers preceding the description of eggs show the extremes, with the size of the normal clutch in parentheses.

I am thankful to several people for their assistance in the preparation of this book. Some will be found listed in the bibliography, one in particular being Frank M. Chapman who, if I remember rightly, set me on a course of meticulous note-keeping, without which I should never have recalled the incidents described. But it is to Gary Low and his fine brush and pencil that I am most indebted.

The commencement of this project coincided, happily, with the beginning of an investigation by the Ministry of Natural Resources of the Province of Ontario into its wetlands. Results of these studies have been provided me by my son, W. Dan Mansell, manager of the Ministry's Huron District. He also read and commented on pertinent sections. Once again, J. Lloyd Van Camp read portions of the manuscript. Finally, Dr. Burt L. Monroe, Chairman, Checklist Committee, American Ornithologists' Union, very obligingly corrected the nomenclature and arrangement to agree with the revised checklist that is scheduled to appear coincidentally with this book.

Notwithstanding such meritorious help, I alone must accept the burden of any errors.

William C. Mansell

Introduction

The cloying perfume of a rose garden; the earthy smell of land released from winter's bondage; the aromatic nose-tingling of wild mint floating over a meadow; the salty tang of a sea breeze; the sweetness after a summer's rain. I have sampled them all. But the incomparable smell is the stinking fragrance of a marsh. A fragrance it is, but one that suggests decay. And though decay means death, we who are privy to the marsh's secrets know full well that the malodorousness originates in a mixture of earth and water which is packed with life; and that means, above all, birth.

There is so much more life in a marsh than anywhere else that any naturalist will include one in his daily peregrinations, preferably visiting it first thing in the morning, anticipating, correctly, that an inevitable change — sometimes subtle, sometimes drastic — will have taken place overnight. The change, however slight, will be one he would like to record in his notebook. In my early birding days, I invariably headed for the depths of the forest in the mistaken belief that many kinds of birds would be sheltering in its gloomy, cavernous interior. I soon found otherwise, and now gravitate first to the nearest marsh in the area.

True, a marsh can stink, sometimes offensively. But many marshes have a delicate fragrance, a mixture of the perfume of water lilies and the fishy odor of pumpkinseed; the musky taint of a raccoon mingling with the mere trace of bog rosemary; pickerelweed and arrowhead struggling to overcome the stench of decay rising from the bloated carcass of a defunct muskrat. Just as ill-tasting bugs are strikingly marked to warn birds of their poor flavor, perhaps marshes smell badly to warn us away, for the bottom is often treacherous, a gumbo that clings with utmost affection to any kind of footgear; and the affection of some kinds of marshes is sometimes fatal. Death may lurk there, but also life. Marshes are the birth place and the nursery of more forms of life per acre than any other kind of topography or habitat. It is to stress the need for their continuity and the consequent preservation of their inhabitants that this book has been written.

The Birth of a Marsh

A marsh is a topographical development, a stage between a lake and a climax forest. The lake itself will have been born by some catastrophic upheaval that created a depression in which water accumulated, introduced by tributary streams and rivers. In the northern hemisphere, most such depressions or pockets were gouged by glacial action.

The lake begins in an oligotrophic state, a pristine condition enjoyed by few bodies of water in today's world. Lake Superior meets this high standard, closely followed by Lakes Huron and Michigan. An oligotrophic lake loses its purity not through pollution, but through conditions arising naturally, for no one lake can remain cold, clear and relatively unproductive indefinitely. Nutrients missing in its newborn state will be added by the streams, creeks and rivers that carry into it the materials such as nitrogen and phosphorus that will increase the lake's fertility. The process may take centuries, but each added bit of nutrient matter will permit increased growth of plant and animal life. Those organisms, minute as they are in the beginning, attract larger forms of life that subsist by devouring them. The prey pass through the alimentary canals of the predators, to be expelled as excrement, and are joined on the lake bed by those few organisms privileged to die of old age.

One way or the other, an increasing number and diversity of forms of life end on the bottom of the lake which, aided by silt brought down by its tributaries, becomes increasingly mucky, increasingly plant-grown and increasingly able to support an abundance of animal life. Gradually, the lake fills in, rising from the bottom as well as drawing inward from the shores, until we have a pond rather than a lake, on its way to becoming a marsh. Of course, if the original depression had been shallow rather than the huge gouge that is Lake Superior, we would have started with a pond, and the filling in would have been accomplished more quickly.

As the lake becomes shallower its waters become warmer, effecting a change in its inhabitants. Bass, sunfish and perch — the fish of warmer waters — replace trout, whitefish and sturgeon, all cold-water fishes; and more and more shoreline becomes grown with shallow-water plants. In the course of time, countless in man's estimation, the lake, doomed from the very beginning, has become a marsh.

But a lake may begin in another way. A piece of the retreating glacier may have broken off to be buried in the sand, gravel and debris left behind by its calving parent. This ice block would melt in the long passage of time, leaving a deep basin of water with usually neither inlet nor outlet. Without the normal inflow of nutrients, such "kettle-hole" lakes lead a more sterile life, become highly acidic through poor drainage, and attract a quite different and smaller plant and animal community. But eventually, even this type of lake will fill in, to become what we call a bog.

There was a time when a marsh meant a wet area grown with low, emergent vegetation; a bog meant a wet area covered by mats of floating vegetation; and a swamp meant an area grown with trees standing in water. All those words are now gathered under the all-embracing term "wetlands," which because of their importance and fragility, have been subjected to intense study universally. Unfortunately, each study-group has evolved its own definitions and terms for each variant of wetlands. Perhaps a modern-day Linnaeus will bring uniformity to the chaotic conditions of definitions and nomenclature. This book ignores the multiplicity of terms and definitions and confines the terminology to marsh, bog and swamp. All three contain land that is wet, most if not all the time.

Just as a lake changes from an oligotrophic state to a marsh, so does one form of wetland change into another form. The transformation is called "succession," with one kind of plant/animal community succeeding another, but so imperceptibly that a wetland once viewed by your grandfather will look the same when seen by your grandchildren.

Although the longevity of man does not permit an individual to conduct a time-study of a wetland, with its inevitable change, it is possible to trace these changes by walking into, or out of, a marsh.

Since a lake diminishes, both vertically and laterally, the first evident step toward becoming a marsh takes place in the shallows formed along the shore receiving the predominant wind, with the resulting waves and drift. We can, therefore, start on the windward shore of almost any body of water and trace the process by wading, then walking, and finally swimming through — more properly, over — a variety of zones, each one forming, by itself, a wetland in its own right.

Before donning waders, snorkel or aqualung, we can stand at the edge of a lake and, looking out toward its deeper parts, see nothing but a watery expanse — black, blue or green, depending on the nature of the bottom and its distance from the surface, on the color of the sky, and on the amount of sunlight at that particular time. Although we may visualize fishes weaving the unfathomable depths, the fish will actually be over shoals, with but a few kinds, such as ling or suckers, foraging at the extreme bottom. That silt-and-muck-covered extremity will have a layer of leaves, leaves we saw floating gaily on the surface all the preceding autumn. It has seemed to me that whenever I trolled too deeply in our lake, which lies in the rocky Muskoka District of Ontario, I snagged sodden leaves; and although I would occasionally hook an old log and, even less frequently, a lake trout, never would I fasten onto a rock, so deep is that leaf cover. Microscopic plant and animal life would be there, consuming the deceased organisms and excrement from living ones, mixing both with detritus building up on the bottom.

The greater the depth, the greater the deficiency in oxygen, with a consequent change in organisms capable of dwelling in that oxygen-deficient world. But, as we cruise outward with snorkel or aqualung, we can see animals, such as snails, clams and other mollusks. A patch of waterweed might be visible, or perhaps a large bed of these plants, the tops sometimes close enough to the surface to caress our knees.

Reversing direction and beginning where the bottom is discernible from shore when the light is favorable, we can see the first plants in the long succession to dry land. The floating, orbicular leaves of water lilies or of spatterdock testify to an exceedingly mucky, uninviting bottom. Pickerelweed, preferring to stand up to its knees in water, may be next, with the spear-shaped leaves of arrowhead still closer to shore. There is no inviolable rule about this, as one plant is successful where another finds colonizing too difficult. It will usually be possible to paddle or at least pole a canoe in these waters, which are inviting to coots, pied-billed grebes, the so-called dabbling ducks, and black terns, and where long-legged herons may stalk finny prey.

Passing from such navigable waters, although progress may be hampered by plant growth, we find ourselves barred or surrounded by a reed-swamp, the first wetland to be dignified by a name shorn of artificiality. The plants, growing in water as much as five feet deep and sending bayonet leaves skyward in stiff array, are bulrushes, attended by some grasses and sedges, all protecting submerged bladderwort. Birds and fishes found in the lily-pad areas may also appear in the open channels and avenues here; and, feeling more secure in the reedy concealment, will move about less cautiously. The reedy growth, breaking up the force of waves and currents, allows an increasing amount of sediment to settle on the bottom, thus gradually reducing the depth of the water. As the water becomes shallower, either because of the rising bottom or closer proximity to the shoreline, there is a gradual reduction in the quantity of reedy growth, until we find our feet, while still wet, are no longer submerged. Now we are in a marsh, the wetland with the greatest and most diverse plant and animal life. Grasses and sedges are numerous; sweet gale, willow and spireae may be present, while a hummock may support a cedar or two. The marsh wren of the cattails will be replaced by the sedge wren; coots by gallinules; and ducks by rails. Some of the replacements will also be found where cattails root just below the water table which, in the marsh, lies at or just below land level.

Where the water table is visible only in spring floods and the silting is but an annual affair, the drier soil, deep, black and rich, attracts willows, red osier dogwood, alders, bog laurel and buttonbush. Yellow warblers and alder flycatchers are now the avian rule, all inhabiting what is called a carr. Penetration is possible but difficult, not only because of the tangle of stems but because the root system of the shrubs persists in snaring an unwary boot.

If the carr is sufficiently drained, or if build up of soil continues, the water table will now be so low (that is, so far below the soil) as to merely keep the soil more or less permanently moist. We will now be in a wooded swamp which, while periodically flooded, will dry out in summer and thus permit the growth of silver and red maples, black ash, tamarack and cedar. In such an environment will be found prothonotary warblers, yellow-throated vireos and blue-gray gnatcatchers; and here, in May and June, will be heard the unducklike "oo-eek" of the wood duck, the male of which Linnaeus traduced with the name "Bride."

If the quality of the marshland or carr soil increases in organic material, the soil will become mucky or peaty. With poor drainage, it will never dry out. It will also remain low in oxygen. In its various degrees of productivity, such a wetland is called a peatland, a fen or an alkaline bog. Sedges and grasses grow profusely here, the former sometimes mixing with cattails or bulrushes. If the rate and flow of water is reduced, thus reducing also the amount of calcium carbonate carried with it, peat submerges the water table still further, increasing its acidity as a result.

Specialists have categorized six kinds of fens, each being less rich than its predecessor, the ultimate one a bog so poor in nutrients it is therefore sparsely inhabited by plants, birds or mammals. Orchids, iris, butterworts, *spirea alba*, bilberry and cranberry and some of our rarer plants grow in the richer fens. The poorer or raised bogs, receiving their water only from rainfall, support only shrubs like Labrador tea or leatherleaf, *Ilex verticillata*, mountain holly, chokeberry, and flowers such as pitcher plant and loosestrife. The muskeg of much of northern Canada is this kind of bog.

The birth of a salt marsh is much the same as that of one of fresh water except that parturition is effected not in a lake but at the edge of a sea, with quite different plants being involved. The area must be relatively quiet, an inlet or a shore sheltered by an island from the force of waves. Silt may be deposited there by a river or creek, or by the constant flow and ebb of tides and waves. Eelgrass, a submergent, keeps filling in such bays and inlets, much to the annoyance of harbor masters. The tendency of this plant is to trap an increasing amount of silt and therefore speed up the process of marsh formation. In time, if periodic dredging has not been conducted, muddy islands will appear, islands so influenced by tides and waves that their position, shape and extent are constantly changing. But, on the more protected and therefore more permanent islands, there will appear a scanty covering of a kind of grass that glories in saline conditions.

Once established, this bit of greenery, called saltmarsh cordgrass, develops rapidly and, by trapping silt and dead vegetation among its roots, speedily advances the development and subsequent merging of muddy bars. The saltmarsh cordgrass welcomes the periodic flooding of its muddy domain, but there comes a time when its work as a builder will have engineered its own demise. The elevating of the island or shore will have increased to the point that flooding recurs only during the higher of high tides. Like cattails and bulrushes in a fresh-water reed swamp, the saltmarsh cordgrass dies out or, to be more precise, moves outward, as do their fresh-water counterparts, toward deeper water and away from dry land.

The quite tall saltmarsh cordgrass has not worked in vain. It has prepared the ground for the shorter saltmeadow cordgrass that cannot tolerate the extreme saline conditions favored by its taller brother. Beyond this saltmeadow cordgrass is a rush *Juncus* of the lily order called black grass, its dark green contrasting sharply with the yellow-green of saltmeadow cordgrass; and this, in turn, is a different shade from the saltmarsh variety. Enjoying the same weaker salinity as the saltmeadow cordgrass are glasswort and sea-lavender, some of the first bits of color one meets away from the sea.

The Life of a Marsh

Life, as is generally believed, began in the sea, when optimum conditions arose to produce some single-cell organism, no doubt neither plant nor animal but a member of that third and recently postulated kingdom, *Protista*, which boasts characteristics of both plants and animals. From that minute organism, all else has descended — or ascended, according to your view of life.

Obviously, life continued to develop in the seas which, shallow as they were then, presented much the same conditions and protection as offshore waters today, especially those covering the continental shelf. Plant life must surely have begun and developed at sea margins, and whether as emergents or submergents, it provided inviting refuge for the growing number and diversity of all forms of life — plant and animal, as well as those so confused as to resemble both or neither at the same time. And, like present-day shore plants, they would have made a large contribution to the formation of higher land through their trapping and accumulating of sediment. As marshes, salt or fresh, have been around much longer than deserts or mountains, life in a marsh is much more diverse and complex than elsewhere.

Something approaching the original forms of life live in the water and the ooze of today's marshes. The plant specimens obtain their energy from inorganic forms of nitrates and phosphates, the base of most fertilizers. Those plants relying on bacteria and fungi to break down inorganic forms to organic ones, contain green substances called chlorophylls which, with the help of sunlight and the ingenious mixture of carbon dioxide taken from the air and hydrogen from the water, manufacture glucose. The process culminates in the release of oxygen, so needed by fish and other aquatic organisms.

Terrestrial plants function in the same way, which is why we must water vegetable gardens and flower beds. Animal forms are without this capacity, so in order to obtain the energy they require, some eat the plants while others eat the plant eaters or consume each other. In any case, the size of the forms will range from microscopic, like amoebae, to huge, such as sequoia trees, elephants and blue whales.

Each kind of life eats only certain other kinds of life. These various dependencies are called food chains. With very few exceptions, the components of each chain will have connections with other chains, so that the whole resembles the web of a spider, and is appropriately called a food web.

The reduction of any of the communities by the removal of one species, by extinction or by extirpation, can mean the demolition of at least a small part of a web, therefore endangering the well-being of an inestimable number of other forms of life that exist as part of that web. The number, diversity and complexity of the forms of life in a marsh are so great that destruction of but a small part of this highly specialized habitat will endanger the longevity of the species of life, plant or animal, contained in that marsh.

In terms of productivity, a marsh is fantastic. Productivity is measured by determining the dry weight of all living things produced in any area. This so-called biomass is, in a marsh, three to four times that of lakes and streams, and three times that of agricultural land. It has been calculated that one salt marsh estuary provides food for two-thirds of the fish and shellfish removed by local commercial fishermen. As for a comparison with agricultural land, tidal marshes are four times as productive as a corn field and six times that of a wheat field, all without an application of one ounce of fertilizer. A marsh, remember, grows its own.

The yield of a corn field can be seen, even before the ears are gathered. But, unfortunately, a marsh, fresh or salt, gives no visual evidence of its value. It appears to be a watery expanse of rushes, cattails, cordgrass, pondweeds, burweeds and water lilies. There may be no evidence of animal life. Yet in one year, one acre of a small salt marsh will produce 100,000 pounds of glucose. The glucose provides food, directly and indirectly, for the diverse aquatic forms of life in the surrounding waters. The energy so produced falls to the marsh bottom and is either converted to detritus or dissolved in water. As this transfer of energy cannot be seen, the uninformed regard a marsh as completely worthless, a view that could be changed quickly if a tasty clam could be seen actually standing on its foot while contentedly munching on a blade of cordgrass.

It is the detritus and algae cultivated in a marsh which is the food of the menhaden and other small fish that breed there; which, in turn, feed the flounder, bluefish and striped bass that grace our table or test mediocre angling skills. These fish, in turn, comprise the diet of such popular game fish as the marlin, sailfish, swordfish and tuna. Indeed, were it not for marshes in Florida's estuaries, we would not enjoy one of the world's epicurean delicacies, shrimp from the Gulf of Mexico. Eliminate the marsh and you reduce man's food supply. When the Netherlands increased its living space by filling in the Zuider Zee, it cut off a principal food source, as that body of water was once one of the world's greatest fisheries.

A friend who found navigation in his lake difficult because of thick beds of weeds, asked me if it were possible to remove them. I assured him that he could do so with the application of a newly concocted compound that killed water weeds. But first, he would require the consent of other residents on the lake; and second, he would have to become inured to unrewarding fishing.

Those weeds growing in a shallow bay well on the way to becoming a marsh provided, I explained, food and shelter for innumerable small fish (minnows and young of larger fishes); shellfish (snails); and crustaceans (crayfish); as well as insects and their larvae. All are relished by bass, sunfish and perch, the fish found in my friend's lake; and by pike, pickerel, muskellunge, walleye and the several kinds of trout found in nearby waters. A fresh-water marsh already formed has an even greater capacity to produce food — morsels that find their way, in due course, into the maws of game fish.

Fishermen are not the only benefactors of marshes. Hunters and trappers would be sore-pressed to find game if marshes ceased to be. Just as small organisms find food and shelter in the submerged parts of plants, so do ducks find shelter, food and nesting sites in the emergent portions. Some will even find refuge in the submerged plants, clinging to them while hunters search the surface in vain for the one they were sure was hit. A large reason for the decrease in the number of ducks in eastern North America is the reduction in the size and number of eastern marshes. A lesser but still highly important factor is the conversion of the many "potholes" of the midwest to agricultural land. Those potholes and sloughs, in reality one vast marsh, are home to innumerable ducks. When I, an easterner and accustomed to seeing but a brood or two on the marshes near my home, saw the number of broods on just one western slough, I needed no computer to determine how the draining of one pothole would affect the duck population of North America.

The inhabitants of marshes range from ubiquitous to unique. Some, like the beaver and muskrat, are unconscious of barriers, moving about freely to settle in unpopulated areas. Others, such as the apple snail, are much more if not wholly sedentary. Their existence is at the mercy of man; and he, with his growing numbers, poses a continued threat to the continuity of wetlands. If the destruction of marshes were to cease, many endangered species would not face the spectre of extinction.

The Death of a Marsh

The king is dead! Long live the king!

When I was quite young, the absurdity of this statement sent me to my father for an explanation. I could not understand why you should plead for the longevity of one who has just expired.

Dad's reply, which after all these years I cannot remember verbatim, boiled down to this: The object of the statement is to provide continuity of succession. The king who has lived up to now no longer lives. After an interval no greater than the width of the period ending this sentence, a plea is raised for the continued health of the old boy's successor. There is, therefore, no perceptible break in the monarchistic rule.

In the same way, one kind of plant growth or wetland succeeds another, merging so successfully that no line of demarcation can be drawn. This will be evident if we begin at the water lilies, walk shoreward, then head on through the various stages of wetland development on both sides of the shoreline and eventually arrive at the climax forest beyond. But we can also trace this succession in another way. Build a platform in a reedswamp, equip it with all the amenities of life including a good stock of food, and lie back to watch the reedswamp change, over the course of several centuries, to a marsh, fen, bog, wooded swamp — to finally become a climax forest.

A marsh dies only to be reborn in an adjacent quarter. It may even seem to walk there. In time, though, it is quite defunct, its parent pond or lake completely filled in and a part of the climax woods of that particular region. But the cycle will start anew elsewhere. Earthquakes and volcanoes; land-, rock- and mud-slides; and fens begun in a natural way — all will change the course of rivers and streams, thus forming new ponds and, in time, bringing about new marshes. Nature refuses to let us down. And where she cannot do it on her own, she enlists the help of beaver who, by diverting or damming waters, create beaver ponds that become beaver meadows that become beaver swamps.

Unfortunately, in arranging for the demise of wetlands, nature has an unwanted assistant who, though eager to play mortician, has no desire to serve also as midwife. Far better termed adversary, he is the greatest loam arranger of all: Man.

To be absolutely fair, a great deal of his works, whether with terra firma or animal life, have been quite justifiable, moves necessary to house, feed and clothe a growing multitude. After all, man persisted in following the Biblical injunction — to the letter — of going forth and multiplying like rabbits.

Therefore, the criticisms, leveled against our forefathers for sending the passenger pigeon into oblivion and almost doing the same with the bison, is unjust. Both were manna in a land frought with hardships. Had our forebears acted with greater restraint, viewing the vast flocks and herds as a finite resource, our criticism might be less harsh. But, rest assured, plane travel would be an extremely hazardous undertaking if passenger pigeons existed in even a fraction of their former numbers; while farming and the maintenance of homes and roads in the plains region would be extremely costly if herds of thousands of bison still roamed freely.

Apathy toward wetlands was shown by man even in earliest times. The lifelessness of a bog, the gloom of a swamp, the scum of algae and duckweed on the waters of a marsh, the swarms of biting insects frequenting all, suggested better living conditions could be found elsewhere. The flickering lights sometimes seen over marshland at night were attributed to the supernatural, and because spirits and devils were undesirable neighbors, wetlands were even more unattractive. The inhospitable atmosphere of a large bog in southern Ontario so affected the original surveyor more than a century ago that he, a devout Roman Catholic, could think of no more suitable name than East and West Luther.

The rich soil of peatland makes the growing of vegetables a comparatively easy matter but tree culture is a different matter. The constant and expensive drainage required renders silvaculture economically unfeasible except for white cedar and black spruce. The latter is the tree of northern bogs and the objective of the pulp and paper industry of northern Ontario. However, no tree farm as yet competes with the natural growth of the north. Peat is also mined, both for a fuel and, after certain refinements, as a potting soil. As neither venture is an economic success, the wetland is worth much more when left in its natural state.

The loss of our wetlands began with the first settlements, as early homesteaders had little use for these waste places. The initial removals were doubtless beneficial, as wetland drainage was necessary to open up the country for tillage and to improve living conditions by removing the breeding grounds of insect pests. Later, wetlands were thought to be impediments to building roads — straight ones, that is — and railways which, if they did not skirt them, virtually destroyed the wetlands by bridging them with embankments. Some were dredged to make or improve harbors, most of which were necessary in early times.

To be economically viable today, a wetland drained for market gardens should have over eight feet of peaty loam. Few peat bogs boast such a depth. Moreover, the additional produce forthcoming from wetlands converted in present times would merely glut the market.

Building thoroughfares over a wetland is almost as harmful as draining it and can be instrumental in causing a disaster. Wetlands team with trees to form nature's defense against flooding; the trees prevent all rain water from reaching the ground at once, the wetlands slow the run-off to watercourses. Moreover, a wetland will improve the quality of the water, which loses impurities as it percolates through the soil. The bog type of wetland can be used as a third-stage filter of sewage waters. The marsh type serves as a catchflow basin for floods as well as a settling pond for sediments. Nothing in nature equals a wetland's ability to recycle nutrients, its stultifying army of bacteria converting dangerous nitrous oxide into the harmless nitrogen form that is 80 per cent of our atmosphere. Nor are the plants of a wetland idle; through photosynthesis, one acre of marshland will produce one pound of oxygen.

The bacteria, algae, duckweed and other low and microscopic forms of plant and animal life found in a marsh all contribute, directly and indirectly, to the higher forms of animate creatures. Fishes like bass, perch, sunfish and catfish are dependent on reedswamps, although they are not often found within them. Some forms of pickerel breed there. Almost all frogs and one or two snakes are found virtually nowhere else. Marshes have varying degrees of appeal to muskrat, beaver, otter, mink and marten. And more than 50 per cent of our birds and almost all our ducks, except oceanic species, use marshes at some time in their lives, nesting and regularly feeding there, or resting as well as feeding during migration.

While humans are obviously dependent on marshes, one marsh is also dependent on another. Without the proximity of other colonies of similar plants, fertilization and seed transfer may be difficult if not completely un-attainable. Thus, the elimination of particular marshes can mean that certain species of plants could become extinct, through their inability either to find partners in the pollination process or to find areas for reestablishment.

A most annoying feature of wetlands is their propensity to produce generations of mosquitoes. Although I have long been aware of the close connection between mosquitoes and marshes, it was only recently that I became acquainted with a certain aspect of this affinity. I was walking over a bush road to an Ontario marsh in the last week of August. Mosquitoes had almost disappeared, even from the wetter parts of the woods. The walk seemed interminable, with no change of habitat to signify that I was nearing my objective, but just as I was beginning to wonder if I would ever reach the place, I found I had company — mosquitoes. Their number was considerably down from the legions of June and July but still enough to be discomforting, and to raise the suspicion, soon confirmed, that the marsh was not much farther on.

With the advent of DDT, it was thought that the mosquito scourge could be eliminated, an idea brought to a halt with the discovery of the harmful effects of DDT on very desirable forms of life. It has been found that the saltmarsh mosquito — there is none more pestiferous — can be controlled by flooding the marsh at an appropriate time. The insects' eggs, which are laid in the wet soil of the marsh, are destroyed through drowning. Provided the disappearance of the mosquitoes does not affect the food supply of other forms of life, it can be seen how easily one pest can be controlled without damaging others.

Indiscriminate or faulty spraying of a marsh can result in disaster. A number of years ago a southern marsh was sprayed with dieldrin, sandflies being the objective. But the aim was off, the sandflies were missed, and almost all fish died instead. Then fiddler crabs, attacking the rotting carcasses, ingested the poison and they, too, were lost. Just one more example of how the gossamer threads of a food-web can be destroyed when man endeavors to eliminate one form of wildlife, which insects are, bringing death to a marsh.

The Rebirth of a Marsh

Recently published figures on the disappearance of marshes are mind-boggling. Of the 5.7 million acres of wetlands once found in southern Ontario, 2.5 to 2.9 million acres have been cleared. I can see, very quickly, that almost half have vanished. Some areas of the province, renowned in the past for their marshes, now boast only a small percentage of the original. The area about Lake St. Clair has lost 39 per cent; 43 per cent of them have disappeared from the north shore of Lake Ontario; and the staggering sum of 75 per cent are gone from the Kawartha Lakes region. This latter, at the edge of the Laurentian Shield, is part of the cottage country, an area under constant pressure, marsh-wise, as cottagers tidy-up small marshy spots about their properties.

In all, Ontario has lost from one-half to three-quarters of all its wetlands. We may view this figure with complacency, however, when it is realized that the largest part of the loss has been to agriculture. (A lesser but still significant loss has been to the formation of the earliest harbors, and some wetlands have given way to the establishment of estate residences.) But our equanimity is severely jolted when we find that not all such conversions to farmland were long-lasting, some being abandoned in short order to become scrubby areas of far less importance than the original. Throughout the world, 100 million acres of wetlands have been lost in the past 75 years.

We also view with dismay the trend to destroy a marsh simply for the pursuit of pleasure. The proximity of many marshes to navigable waters, the apparent worthlessness of such wetlands, and the ease with which they can be dredged immediately suggests to the yachting fraternity their conversion to marinas. It cost more than three million dollars to save one Lake Ontario marsh from such a fate, while the battle over another continues.

It is more than a hopeful proposition that if an area was wetland once, it usually can be a wetland again. All that may be required is to let nature take over, provided the principal ingredient it must work with is clean, pure water. But if nature's method of getting water to and holding it in that area has been thwarted, man must give her a helping hand.

One way is to dam a watercourse and flood otherwise useless land. One of Ontario's largest and best wetlands is Luther Marsh, near Orangeville. The damming of Black Creek there created a 16,200-acre reservoir which is rimmed with cattails and bulrushes. Ducks began breeding in such quantity and quality as to throw consternation into those whose painstaking work preparing breeding ranges was rendered obsolete. In addition to providing a new habitat for ducks, ospreys, waders and shorebirds, a reservoir was created and flood control established. A similar and subsequent undertaking, involving the corners of three Ontario counties (Wellington, Wentworth and Halton) gave birth to Mountsberg Reservoir, which while less marshy than Luther, is still a haven for all manner of water birds. Diefenbaker Lake was created in Saskatchewan in the same way, with, from my brief examination, gratifying results.

A more expensive way to re-create a marsh is to plant thousands of aquatic plants after waters have been dammed or diked. Such a step is not always necessary but it does help. In any event, it speeds up restoration.

It would seem, then, that far from being the trash lands viewed by so many, wetlands have an incalculable value. Consider:

Their use by waterfowl for nesting and, especially in the migration season, for resting and feeding.

Their use by important fur-bearers such as muskrat, beaver, otter, mink and marten.

Their use by larger game mammals such as moose and deer.

Their serving as natural reservoirs.

Their serving as natural flood controls.

Their ability to absorb an astounding amount of sewage, thus producing oxygen and nitrogen.

Their ability to improve the quality of water.

Their use in recreational pursuits such as hunting and fishing.

Their use for recreational purposes such as birdwatching, a widely abused but not quite truthful ploy to convince politicians of the need for retaining wetlands in their original state.

In the final analysis, Henry Ward Beecher summed it up very nicely when he said: "We would so live and labor in our time that what came to us as seed may go to the next generation as blossom, and that which came to us as blossom may go to them as fruit."

detail:
American Bittern
page 29

Pied-billed Grebe

Podilymbus podiceps

Breeds from the tree line in Canada south to Argentina in South America. Winters in the southern tier of states in the U.S. south through Central America and northern South America.

Four items from my notebooks describe this distant relative of the loons very well. They begin with the first time I ever saw one.

"September 26, 1934: I had just passed the Old Mill bridge, on my way north, and was in the vicinity of the sewer outlet, when I saw what at first seemed to be a snake swimming in the water. Then it disappeared and I suspected a grebe. I waited some time and saw nothing. I thought it had possibly swum under water and taken refuge under the foliage on the opposite bank; so I searched that shore and waited quietly. Soon it came out, to swim and dive not twenty feet from me."

A chickenlike white bill, yes, but a snaky profile if just the head is showing. And a penchant for diving, not to the nether regions but to a cover of emergent vegetation, where it remains quite concealed.

"October 9, 1936: This morning I saw one trying to take off from lower Grenadier Pond. It pattered over the water like a loon, its feet moving, I believe, alternatively, and in unison with the wing-beats. I also saw them on the water, with the head submerged, looking below like a loon."

Loonlike, you see, with the same difficulty of becoming airborne.

"October 31, 1937: Frank Cook, Doug Miller and I saw one that bobbed up in the Humber, just below Bloor Street, 100 feet from us. It went down, came up again, then, seeing us, seemed to arch its back, stretch the neck and tail and, in that position, sink, to be seen no more."

This could only have been an elaborate version of its ability to sink without effort, something I saw in a more normal way ten months later, about 100 yards farther north.

Thirty-four years later, on July 29, 1972, my dog Skerry was the victim of a wasp, so I headed for a nearby lake to let him dunk his sting. As he entered the water I saw a single pied-bill about 100 yards offshore. While the dog swam I stood quietly. "I was now aware that the grebe was much closer, seeming very interested in the proceedings. So I began giving it all my attention, standing motionless. It would dive, reappear in a spot ten or fifteen feet removed, circle a bit, eying Skerry all the while; then it would dive again, to reappear a little closer. It continued in that fashion until within thirty feet of us, when Skerry came out of the water. The whole show, I suppose, was a form of tolling."

Tolling, with a dog or even a bright rag, is an old method of enticing ducks within shooting range. Perhaps it is efficaceous with all swimming birds, as I have had loons approach me closely when I have been wading in shallow water.

I would have qualms about wading or swimming out to pied-bills, as the cool, clear water frequented by loons is not for grebes. Their preference is muck-bottomed, weed-grown ponds, or marshes with open water or "canals," all presenting the vegetation they both nest in and hide in.

Both loons and grebes pay dearly for their versatility on and under water, being almost if not completely incapable of walking. The pied-bill seems more accomplished than others, progressing in a sort of crouch or labored run. But, if pressed, it abandons the text "How to Walk in Ten Easy Lessons," and, lying on its breast,

moves feet and wings as if swimming. Also common to both loons and grebes is the free transportation parents offer their young, allowing the children to ride on their backs.

Except in fall and late winter, when concentrations of as many as twenty-five will be found in more open waters, pied-bills are quite secretive. Thus, when you first hear someone calling up a lost cow, there is nothing to associate the sound with a bird of any kind. The notes, though, constitute the pied-bill's song, a well-enunciated series *cow, cow, cow, cow, cow, cow, cow,*

beginning low and soft, with an increase in volume and tempo, to fade away at the end. The closing notes, with a rising inflection, sound like *cow-uh, cow-uh, cow-uh*. It gives other sounds, all in keeping with its marshy surroundings.

Nest: A dishlike mound of decayed vegetation and mud, built up from the bottom, floating freely or anchored to vegetation. Eggs: 4-8 (4-6, normal), greenish- or bluish-white, soon becoming nest-stained, elliptical to subelliptical, smooth. Single-brooded. Incubation: 22-23 days, by both sexes. Food: Insects, crustaceans, fishes.

Eared Grebe

Podiceps nigricollis

Breeds in the prairie region of southern Canada and the northern U.S. Winters in southwestern U.S. south to South America. Also breeds and winters in the Old World.

Black-necked grebe is a far better name for this almost circumpolar species, which has been known by that name in Great Britain since Hablizl described it in 1783. It has no more visible ears than the horned grebe, its close relative, has goatlike adornments. It does sport, in summer, a golden corn-tassel that fans from back of the eye and covers the auricular region, where the real ears lie behind black feathers. The screech, great horned and long-eared owls lead you more astray with their "ear" tufts.

This bird has no regard for people who like to draw neat distribution maps, and even less for those who are given to expostulating some theory of range expansion. In a way it is circumpolar, although nesting well south of the tundra. But it disdains the eastern half of the USSR and possibly all of China; nor does it venture east of the Manitoba-Ontario boundary line in Canada or its extrapolation in the United States. So, where did it originate and how and why did it cross an ocean and a half-continent to colonize elsewhere?

In North America its favorite areas for nesting are the numerous sloughs of the western prairies; and as most of these sloughs are shallow with at least their borders marshy, the eared grebe thrives, nesting in solitary fashion if the slough is but a pothole but gathering in hundreds if the watery expanse justifies the description, "lake." Others of the two diving orders, the loons and the grebes, are reluctant to place their nests in public places. Not so our spray-eared grebe. It will nest under marshy cover but is more in-

clined to locate in open water, though at least far enough from shore to keep you at a safe distance. I have seen some Alberta sloughs so punctuated with grebe nests, all looking like inflated tires anchored for boat mooring, that I think I could have hop-scotched across the water without wetting my feet.

Well, keeping my feet nearly dry, as, like others of this order, the eared grebe is a poor artisan, content with a heap of soggy vegetation, building it up either from the bottom or right on the surface of the water when this heap is anchored to growing reeds. The platform is so unstable that the incubating bird, returning after a forced or voluntary rest period, clambers aboard so carelessly that an egg or two sometimes rolls into the water. Given enough warmth in that element the eggs might still hatch, as most nests are so waterlogged that the eggs they contain are partly in water at all times anyway. Small wonder the young can swim and dive the instant they leave the egg.

The courtship antics of eared grebes are as entertaining as those of the large western grebe, which is found, in smaller numbers, on the same waters. Races take place but not in the spectacular fashion of the larger bird. The eared is more given to a "penguin" dance, splashing vigorously while facing a partner and even touching breast to breast. Head-wagging is another common display, but it is not yet known whether this signals refusal or the amazement of one bird at having won such a beautiful spouse.

Eared grebes tend to be more clannish than horned grebes, wintering in flocks of not only hundreds but up to a half-million birds, which staggering figure is found in the Salton Sea of mid-southern California.

But whether in the Old or the New World, the

G. LOW 83 -

eared grebe engages in no adventurous travel, rarely touring the country to the east or southeast of its birthplace. The species does seem to be popping up in eastern North America more frequently of late, but the increased number of sightings must be tempered by the greater proficiency and number of observers, few of whom could be as stupid as this one.

Just nine days before penning this, my wife and I were at Port Dover, on Lake Erie, finding but a large semicircle of open water off the port entrance, partly rotten ice elsewhere. A grebe, diving repeatedly at the west side of the half-circle, caught our eyes, but other than prompting a comment that it was a bit early for a horned grebe, elicited no further response. Anyway, the wind was chill and damp and the warmth of the car was a more powerful magnet than a colorless, patternless diver, too far away to yield good field marks. It was while studying color plates preparatory to writing this that I wondered if I had made a goof, for a difference in outline persisted in my memory.

The horned and eared grebes are easily differentiated when in the nuptial plumage but, unless at close range, are distinguished with difficulty at other times. Both are dark-gray above, white below, with a number of subtle differences most of which are matters of degree. One is that the carriage of the eared is more upright, which is how my wife and I recalled our bird. The others are: The bill of the eared is wider than high at the base and is slimmer and seems upturned; the forehead is more abruptly vertical; the neck is thinner and straighter, again seemingly featured by our bird; the back is more rounded with the stern seeming to ride higher; the eared is grayer and darker, especially on the foreneck where it is virtually gray; the dark cap is ill-defined, extending to below the eyes where it merges into the grayer cheeks; a white patch is usually on the ear region, while the eye itself is redder. My one excuse is that I was not familiar with the winter plumage of the eared grebe, and saw nothing really out of the ordinary, then, to excite me.

The silence of all grebes away from the breeding grounds was another obstacle in identification. To have heard the call would have helped. The usual call of the eared grebe is a *pu-weep*, which, like others of its notes, is given with a rising inflection. The others run from a single-syllabled *kreep* to a *hick-or-ick-up*. A wheezy *wa-waah-wa* is crooned in a monotone.

Nest: A platform of soggy marsh vegetation built up from the bottom or anchored to reeds. Eggs: 2-5 (3-4), white, soon becoming nest-stained, elliptical to subelliptical, smooth. Sometimes two-brooded. Incubation: 21-22 days, by both sexes. Food: Insects, crustaceans and fishes.

Eared Grebe

American Bittern

Botaurus lentiginosus

Breeds from the tree line in Canada south to the middle of the southern U.S. Winters in the lower half of the U.S. and in Central America.

It seems odd to refer to this bird as the "American" bittern. True, it is confined, as a breeding bird, to North America north of Mexico, a range shared with no others of this genus, a not-so-friendly one. Each of its three relatives has a continent or more all its own: South and Central America; Europe, Asia and Africa; and the Australian region. Of its several oddities, though, the most amazing is that the American bittern was first described and named for science from an individual taken in England in 1813. In fact, it is so espoused to the British Isles that it has since been detected there on more than forty occasions. Don't, however, look for an exchange of visits by the Eurasian species as it, like all except a minuscule number of European birds, finds the prevailing westerlies too great a handicap to complete an east-west crossing.

Literature, apart from books dealing with natural history, has many references to the Eurasian species, which differs little from ours in habits. British authors dwell on this bird's liking for inhospitable marshes, swamps and bogs; for its being a pronounced ascetic; and for its peculiar song. A good many poets, who probably had never seen a bittern, enthused over its "booming," sometimes calling it "bellowing," a terminology followed by writers of natural history almost to the present. But British naturalists now compare the song of their bird to a fog horn or the lowing of a cow. Our bird is said to boom, too, but I have heard many cows and have been right beside the light and horn in a lighthouse when the latter was blasting away, and I'm afraid none of my bitterns has sounded bovine or suggested a fog horn.

Indeed, my notes of an American bittern both seen and heard in May, 1942, state that the sound was a *plunk, plunk, plunk*, and had it not been for my having the author in view at the time, I might have put it down as the work of a distant carpenter hammering on wood. This was the only time I attempted to enter its notes in my journals in syllabic English. On all other occasions I followed the time-worn example and simply wrote that I had heard a bittern "booming," being careful, however, to use quotation marks.

Its notes do resemble the sound of a heavy mallet driving a stake into muck; hence the cognomen, "stake-driver." But since there are three syllables given in close succession, there must be either three hammerers involved or someone as hefty as Vulcan doing the job. Others aver the sound is that of an old-fashioned pump in need of a new gasket, or one requiring extra priming to bring the water column to the top. In the opinion of Edward Howe Forbush, both interpretations are correct. He found that when he was on one side of the bird he heard a stake-driver, and when on the other, a faulty pump. Further, far-carrying as the sound may be, the number of syllables heard will be increased by distortion, decreased by distance.

The sound is really an undignified belch on a large scale. First the bird gulps-in air, clicking the bill with each inhalation. Then it releases the air in such volume as to produce the hollow sound. Its various contortions throughout this effort suggest it is suffering extreme pain or nausea. Anyone who has been caught unawares by something more than a genteel burp will agree that the bird may be in pain.

Like the least bittern, with whom it shares

G. LOW 82—

many a marsh, the American bittern is a master in the art of concealment, freezing in the same fashion, yellow eye glaring around a bill pointing skyward. But the variegated plumage of the larger bird blends more perfectly with its reed- and rush-grown habitat. Moreover, it has been seen to sway along with wind-blown vegetation, matching the movement to perfection. The ruse, stationary or otherwise, is an instinctive one; a bird I surprised on a road between marshy areas persisted in trying to emulate a reed clump, the nearest of which was twenty yards distant!

The American bittern is, usually, a lethargic performer afield, standing (it almost never perches) in hunched reverie for long periods. But let an unsuspecting frog or minnow approach and the bird's neck will stretch out ever so slowly until, with lightning speed, a marsh denizen will have become a meal. The same swift stab will be directed to the eyes of an intruder who manages to get within arm's-length of the bird. If fishing is poor at one spot, it will travel to another location in the same marsh with the most exasperating deliberation. Yet it does not always watch its step, as I saw one slip from flattened cattails at the edge of a canal into deep water, where it swam with the aplomb of a duck.

As it is a much larger bird than the least bittern, it is seen more easily and therefore with greater frequency; and as it is less enamored of one particular marsh, it is seen more often in flight than is the smaller bird. In flying between hunting grounds, the American bittern has the aspect of a very dark heron with quite black wing tips; but the flight, although slow, is accom- plished with stiffly held wings beating more rapidly than a heron's. On being flushed from its retreat, its initial effort, like that of a great blue, is an ungainly one, and is accompanied by a harsh, nasal *krawk*.

The American bittern hunts wherever ground is wet underfoot, yet will visit dry fields where grasshoppers abound. It has nested in a clump of tall grass in such situations but prefers by far the cover provided by the spearlike blades of cattails and bulrushes. It is before such foliage has attained full growth that the bittern reveals an adornment very few people have seen. In his display, which seems to have as its purpose the determination of the sex of the opposing bird, the male uncovers two tufts or a ruff of white feathers that sprout from near each side of the base of the neck. The feathers vary in size with the bird and, throughout the performance, will point to different directions. I have seen them as large as the rim of a fedora, but they are said to be even larger on occasion. If one male fails to outbluff (or outruff?) another, breast-to-breast warring may ensue a few feet off the ground, but the only damage is to dignity.

Nest: A flimsy, slightly hollowed platform of dead marsh vegetation, usually 4 to 5 inches above water but sometimes on the ground and occasionally in a bush. The tops of surrounding reeds may be arched over. Eggs: 2-7 (3-5), olive- brown to olive-buff, nearly elliptical, smooth, slightly glossy. Incubation: 24-29 days, by the female alone. Food: Mollusks, spiders, crusta- ceans, insects, fishes, amphibians, snakes, lizards, small birds and small mammals.

Least Bittern

Ixobrychus exilis

Breeds east of the Great Plains in the U.S. and in the southern triangle of Ontario south to Central America. Winters in the southern U.S. south to northern South America.

When I prepared to write this essay, I wondered who, of all ornithologists, was most qualified to do so. For this bird, our smallest heron, is so secretive, so furtive, so wedded to inhospitable wetlands densely grown with cattails, reeds and sedges, that it is unknown even to some advanced birders. What little we know of its life history is a compendium of effort, attended largely by good fortune, of ornithologists — from lucky amateur to case-hardened pro — scattered throughout the Americas.

It has never been postulated, nor is it here, that the least bittern is a link connecting herons and rails. But with a little imagination, one can visualize the transmigration of the characteristics of, say, a Virginia rail to the heronlike features of the little bittern; and thence to those typical of our larger and more familiar herons. Or, of course, it may be your pleasure to proceed from the great blue heron through this bittern to the Virginia and other rails.

The bittern and rails do have some things in common. They skulk in a habitat that extends little welcome to man. They announce their presence by a variety of calls attributed to other kinds of birds, mammals and even frogs. If your fortitude and equipment permit penetration of their mysterious haven, sending the birds into startled flight, all will convey the impression that the air is, to them, a foreign element, attested by dangling legs and a weak, fluttering effort. Never do they fly far, covering not more than a few yards before dropping back into the dank, dark recesses they love. Nothing short of a roaring conflagration will put them up a second time.

If it is your wish to see this Wizard of Ooze, retire to some marsh in early May, when withered rushes still prostrate themselves to the devasting force of winter. Sit, now quietly, and very, very patiently. Your reward may be a foot-long bird of heron-form marked in solid patches of browns and ochers. It will tread cautiously, its head shooting forward with each step. Later, when the marsh vegetation is a phalanx of spears pointing skyward, the bittern may sometimes be seen near the edge, snaking between the stalks like an all-star running back between would-be tacklers. The bittern, though, always scores, even when the obstructions are no more than an inch apart. When soggy land gives way to water, progress is in the same manner unless the depth is too great. Then the bird proceeds by grasping reeds, its speed not one whit diminished.

Startle him and he croaks a harsh *kwah* as he takes labored flight. If your intrusion is near the nest, the bird's displeasure will be announced by a cackling *ka-ka-ka-ka*, which some say resembles the common call of the magpie. The heron-bittern tribe is far removed from the songbirds, with none of them exhibiting any musical ability. There is even an absence of resonance in their various alarm calls, all being flat in timbre. But the least bittern does have a song, a series of rapid, low, guttural *coos* so muted as to be scarcely heard above the other noises rising from the marsh. Depending on your reception and distance from the "singer" it may sound like the cooing of a dove, an amorous cuckoo, the love song of a pied-billed grebe or even the croaking of a frog. Some calls seem lifted from coots or mudhens, so the least bittern can sound like an entire marsh itself.

This bittern does not have the patience of the larger herons when hunting, but instead moves about actively, picking up a morsel here, another there, a third elsewhere. But unlike those herons, which take to the air at your approach, the bittern, if it has sufficient warning, will freeze, remaining motionless for many minutes. In the usual frozen posture, the body is compressed, feathers flattened and neck outstretched, the whole topped by a yellow spire — its bill. Although broadly patterned rather than streaked, the bird nevertheless merges perfectly with the surrounding grasses. If you move around quietly, its neck will turn sufficiently in order to keep its baleful, unblinking eyes full on you. Even while you watch, it may move backward to vanish in uncanny fashion; and unless you make a sudden move yourself, it will reappear in the same ghostly way. One I watched hunting spotted a victim and immediately froze in what seemed to be a most awkward position. But, some minutes later, when its prey moved a little closer, the bird's neck uncoiled with a grace belying cramps, and some marsh inhabitant became an entrée.

An intriguing feature of the least bittern is the differently colored costume that some sport, with the lighter areas replaced by a dark, rich brown. The darker bird was once deemed a separate species called Cory's bittern *(I. neoxena)*, but the costume is now considered to be a color phase; yet arguments still go on. Most of the specimens taken also show an intrusion of white feathers, and as P. A. Taverner pointed out, albinism, erythrism and melanism would not likely occur in the same individual, giving credence to its being a full species. Arthur C. Bent refers to the findings of Oscar E. Baynard, who averred that Cory's did not interbreed with the common

form; and that their darker eggs hatched into downy young as black as those of a rail, rather than the normal buff. Perhaps, as Taverner suggested, it is a species dying out and which, now, may be extinct. Sixteen of the thirty-one known specimens were taken at Toronto's Ashbridge's Bay, where they nested but can do so no longer as the area has been filled in. Most of the rest were found in Florida, while a few were captured near Lake Erie in Ontario or in the states on or close to that body of water. The last specimen taken was in 1914, and the last reported sighting was at Long Point, Ontario, on September 16, 1928.

As stated at the beginning, sights of this bittern in any color phase fall to the more fortunate, and I have been both lucky and unlucky. At Point Pelee, Ontario, my wife and I were trying to locate the author of some call, finally maneuvering to get the vocalist in between us. Only my wife was looking in the right direction when the bird, a least bittern, rose. I spent the rest of the day explaining the glum countenance I was toting around. But perhaps I have some claim to being more familiar than many others with this bird. On May 21, 1950, when in a marsh near the mouth of the Humber River at Toronto, I watched the weak flight of a Cory's bittern!

Nest: A flat structure of reeds, rushes and sticks supported by marsh vegetation, occasionally arched by bending the tops of rushes; also occasionally in bushes and more rarely on the ground. Eggs: 2-7 (4-5), pale bluish- or greenish-white, elliptical, smooth, non-glossy. Incubation: 16-19 days, by both sexes. Food: Leeches, mollusks, crustaceans, insects, small fish, amphibians, lizards and, occasionally, small mammals.

Least Bittern

Great Blue Heron

Ardea herodias

Breeds from the southern edge of the coniferous belt in Canada south to Mexico and the West Indies. Winters in the U.S. and Central America.

The giraffe is said to have a long neck because its head is so far away from its body, which may be the reason for the length of the neck of a great blue heron. This bird is not blue (bluish-gray, perhaps), but it is certainly great, just slightly inferior to the whooping and sandhill cranes, our largest North American birds.

Yet, although standing four feet high and stretching even taller when launching its huge frame into the air, the rising of one from a small marsh on a golf course went unnoticed by nineteen of twenty golfers, myself being the odd one out. (Under way, its neck is curved back on the shoulders but the long, trailing legs still give it the same length over all.) Given its stature, the great blue is quite capable of stepping from a sandy bottom to a small dock, then down the other side to continue its search for minnows. But the bird of my summer home walked under the dock that rested on water some eighteen inches deep. Imprints of its long, dinosaurlike toes on the sandy bottom about the dock were not surprising; two prints under the dock were eminently so.

It is surprising, too, how many times I have misidentified such a large bird that, usually, is correctly named as far away as I can see it. On one occasion a bird seen on the second last day of the year, two months after its normal departure date, was difficult to identify because of the intervening trees of a wooded swamp. From the white I could see on the head, I insisted it was a Krider's hawk, an observation considerably at variance to the long bill my wife could see and which I could not. Moving cautiously, I saw a great blue in three-quarter profile, head and bill partly screened by a tree-trunk. On another occasion I took one for a red-tailed hawk, and on still another, for an eagle soaring at such great height I could not recognize a heron form and legs until use of my binoculars brought the bird back to earth. Then, near Toronto's International Airport one time I wondered why four planes should be flying in the form of a cross. Their soundless flight suggested gliders but I could not conceive gliders flying in close formation. Four great blue herons finally materialized.

The great blue is found wherever shallow water or marsh vegetation encourages small fish or frogs, or where a meadow houses meadow voles or small birds. Ice-free waters would then be a prerequisite, except that two birds of my acquaintance insisted on being served directly from the refrigerator. One was standing in the water covering the ice of a lake in early spring; the other was on an ice block in winter.

Its size renders it both conspicuous and a target for trigger-happy hunters. (My younger son pointed to two bodies floating a few yards apart on a small lake in rural Ontario.) It is therefore very difficult to get close to a great blue, whose precipitous departure will be accompanied by a harsh *onk*. But there are exceptions. One, resting on the seawall off Toronto's Sunnyside Beach, apparently harbored aspirations of lifeguard duty — the water between it and shore was thronged with bathers. And while a heronry (they nest in colonies) is established in difficult-to-reach places, I was interested to see that a small one

looked down on the thousands of people having fun in Vancouver's Stanley Park.

The heronry, by the way, may contain dozens of nests, young in various stages of development and the carcasses of a few who unwisely abandoned the security of the nest, slipped and either fell to the ground to starve from inattention or hung themselves from the fork of a branch, all adding to the stench of excrement and regurgitated and uneaten food. It is not a place to be visited by the overfastidious or by anyone without an umbrella. But just as some birds prefer fast-frozen foods, so others want to be alone. I was shown a nest, in use then for five years, atop a sign standing in solitary fashion in the middle of the channel of Aransas Bay, Texas.

The great blue is, usually, a loner, associating with others only in the heronry, although very loose flocks of a half-dozen or so may be seen on migration. Birds tend to be well scattered throughout the feeding grounds, with only three or four in sight at one time. In certain localities you can see more. The shallows of Tsawwassen, British Columbia, are irresistible to them. While waiting to board the ferry to Vancouver Island I noted some fifty great blues wading in the salty bay.

Nest: In colonies; a platform of sticks high in trees, but also in bushes or even on the ground when taller growth is unavailable. Eggs: 3-5 (4), pale greenish-blue, oval to subelliptical, smooth, non-glossy. Single-brooded. Incubation: 28 days, by both sexes. Food: Crustaceans, insects, coarse fish, frogs, reptiles, small birds, small mammals.

Great Egret

Casmerodius albus

Breeds from just south of Canada south to the tip of South America and in similar latitudes in the Old World. Winters in the southern U.S. southward.

Since its near extermination around the turn of the century, when it was the millinery trade's unwitting supplier of aigrettes, then the rage of fashion, the great egret has led a prolific existence, recovering not only its old numbers in the south but pioneering settlements northward. When I became interested in birds fifty years ago, records of great egrets about Toronto, Ontario, my home city, totaled three, while the total for the whole province was little more than ten, most of which had been reported from the north shore of Lake Erie. The species may now be accounted regular but rare in that area; very rare at Toronto, and an occasional sight elsewhere in the province north to Lake Nipissing.

In 1937 (October 3 to be exact), on my first visit to Point Pelee, our car had scarcely stopped when I was in rapid transit for its famous marsh, for egrets had been reported there a few days previously. The six birds I found almost immediately were a sight so heartwarming that they tempered the cold, raw wind blowing in off Lake Erie. Five birds huddled as though debating an immediate return to their warm, sunny Florida; the sixth, off by itself, stood erect, defying the chill as if an inveterate fresh-air fiend.

Twenty years later, their distribution differed so little that when tooling through northern Ohio, my wife at the wheel, my usual regard for safe-driving went the way of New Year's resolutions on January 2 when I spotted a "long white" in a marsh. I yelled "Stop!" so loudly and suddenly my wife came close to wrapping us around a tree. The subsequent tongue-lashing I received was duly compensated by the white vision considerably north of its normal range.

The egret is an inveterate post-breeding wanderer. Birds seen north of its breeding range from July on are individuals whom itchy wings have carried to unusual localities, not necessarily north of their natal area. Southbound ocean-crossing seems commonplace at such times. Recent spring records in southern Ontario, however, suggest pioneers are reaching out for still more living room.

In many respects the great white is like a small, albino great blue or a small version of the great white heron, inhabiting the same type of marshy areas, feeding in the same manner, stalking with stealthy strides or waiting with infinite patience. It does, however, greatly outnumber the great blue in coastal waters, yielding to it inland. Even its flight has the same wing-beat, heavy and measured. I once saw what I took to be two great blues dropping to water, so similar were they in form and flight. Then I was pleasantly surprised to find I was only half right, for they landed to reveal one had the all-white form of an egret. Sunlight, glinting from the white bird, had made it look as gray as its companion.

The great white egret is even more globe-trotting than the black-crowned night-heron. In the western hemisphere it breeds from the latitude of Lake Erie south to the tip of South America, absent only in the arid country of the midwest, and even there it winters in the southern portion. In the other hemisphere it is unknown on the African and Australian deserts and the great heights of India, but elsewhere it breeds north to the latitude of the Mediterranean Sea and, in the extreme east, northern Japan.

It nests in colonies, other herons being tolerated, of course. But the usual territorial disputes carry on, no matter which species, if any, are neighbors.

Like other herons, too, it is no vocalist. A low-pitched croak or a series of them is the extent of its vocabulary. But around the nest it attempts a certain levity, a lighter kind of croak suggesting it does find some happiness in, at least, family life.

Nest: In colonies; a flat structure of twigs and sticks, flatter than that of a great blue heron; in trees, usually fairly high up. Eggs: 3-6 (4-5), pale bluish-green, elliptical to subelliptical, smooth. Incubation: 23-24 days, by both sexes. Food: Crustaceans, insects, fishes, frogs and snakes.

Great Egret

G. LOW 83 —

Snowy Egret

Egretta thula

Breeds from the middle of the U.S. south to the middle of South America. Winters in the southern U.S. southward.

Although I have seen hundreds of snowy egrets (but none farther north than New Jersey), I can find nothing in my notes other than repetitions of stereotyped habits already well documented. Certainly I never met a snowy with marked idiosyncrasies. It would seem that if you have seen one short white, as they are described in the deep south, thus differentiating it from the long white or great egret, you will have seen them all.

One must, however, be on guard that it is a snowy you have in view, as white is always in fashion among the heron tribe, whether long, short or otherwise. There is the great white heron of the Florida Keys, yellow of bill and legs, said to be merely a color phase of the great blue heron, a misconception in my humble opinion. There is the great egret, a half-foot shorter than the great white, yellow of bill, black of legs, found throughout the tropical regions of the world. Next in size and a half-foot larger than the snowy, is the white phase of the reddish egret. Its bluish legs and flesh-colored bill, the end half of which is black, differ markedly from the snowy's. It is a shaggier bird as a rule, too. The little blue heron, which is white before maturity, is very close to the snowy in size but has bluish or grayish legs, a bill black at least at the end, and a tinge of blue in the plumage, especially in the long flight feathers. The smaller cattle egret is all white except in the nesting season, when rusty patches are evident on head, breast and back. Its bill may be yellow, orange or black, depending on age and season.

All that variety seems to leave little for the snowy to claim as its own. But it manages to distinguish itself with black legs and incongruously yellow toes, a black bill with only a bit of the base showing yellow, and a plumage that positively glistens, it is so white. It is one of the best-named birds in the world, provided you know what fresh snow looks like. Watch, though, and don't be misled by a young snowy that has not all-black legs but black with the hind edge yellowish.

The yellow toes, yellower than those of the little egret of the Old World, are both fascinating and intriguing. Just when you think you have a white heron with the legs completely black, the bird will take a cautious step revealing toes of a shade that a yellowlegs must envy. Their color must have a purpose, and since the big attraction sexually is the fine plumes worn during the nuptial season, it has been postulated that the only reason for yellow legs can be to attract fish! A plausible theory. The toes also agitate the water, stirring up organisms, but that can be accomplished by toes of any hue.

The snowy is known to agitate not only with its toes but with its whole being, rushing hither and yon as if the pangs of hunger are unbearable. I confess most of the birds I have seen were more sedate than this, but were still much more active than any other heron of any color, most of which are content to emulate a statue while awaiting the incautious approach of some tidbit. The snowy's madcap method of fishing includes throwing up its wings, perhaps to startle a fish or frog into the last move it will ever make. In appearance, its yellow toes set it apart from all others, but one action in particular is characteristic. It is said to hover, petrel-like, over water.

I began this sketch with a résumé of the field

marks of the white herons. You will need them almost constantly, as the snowy rarely moves without company, the little blue and tricolored herons being favorites. It nests in company, too, but is less than tolerant of others — even its own kind — inclined to quarrel almost incessantly with any bird nesting near it.

It is truly a beautiful bird in appearance but far from so vocally, given vent to harsh cries and a grating *aah-aah* which may be lengthened into an *a-wah-wah-wah*. A bubbling *wulla-wulla-wulla* seems quite out of character.

Nest: In colonies; on the ground or in bushes or small trees, or in tules or rushes over water; a platform of sticks lined with finer twigs. Eggs: 3-5 (3-4), pale bluish-green, elliptical, smooth, non-glossy. Incubation: 18 days, by both sexes. Food: Crustaceans, insects, small fishes, and frogs.

Little Blue Heron

Egretta caerulea

Breeds in the Gulf states and south Atlantic states of the U.S. and in Central and South America. Winters in or close to the tropics.

Its name, little blue heron, suggests it is the smallest pea in a pod of blue waders, when in truth it is the world's only truly blue heron. The purple heron of the eastern hemisphere has blue in its back and wings but with an intrusion of reddish imparting the appearance of our great blue after a tumble into a wine vat. The great blue heron and its Eurasian counterpart, the gray heron, are both gray with a tendency to slate rather than to blue.

Except for its dark purple head and neck, the little blue is blue all over, although, like the indigo bunting which is just as thoroughly blue, it will appear all black in certain lights. But, remember, in its immature stage, it does its best to emulate the great and snowy egrets and the white phases of the great blue heron and reddish egret. Actually, the introduction of blue dye rather than bluing into its bath-water has shown that the bird is never immaculate, a trace of blue showing up almost anywhere, but especially at the wing tips. Never does it glisten like the similarly sized snowy. In its final stages of immaturity (a misnomer, as white individuals will breed), little blues show a patch of white here, a little blue there, and that, come to think of it, may be the origin of its name.

When I review my fifty years of bird observations I am always amazed that the seventy-fourth species on my list was a little blue heron, seen on two different occasions at Toronto where, observer-wise, I was only 145 days old. In my ignorance at that time, I accepted the record matter-of-factly, beginning to question it only sometime later, when I knew more of birds and

their distribution. Then, to my intense relief, I discovered that a foremost Toronto observer had seen a little blue heron about the same time and in the same locality as had I. My seventy-fourth species was therefore allowed to stand.

From such intimacy (I had been quite close to my first little blue) I was relegated to the role of a more distant observer as I poked into various marshes from New Jersey down the eastern seaboard to Key West, finding myself in agreement with other writers, who stated that this species prefers fresh water. But it is far from averse to salt water. While it does nest away from the sea, I think most birds are within a day's flight of the oceanside. In fact, in the Florida Keys it is unable to find fresh water anywhere, nor is it much more successful in the Caribbean islands where, at St. Lucia, I saw my most recent little blue, wading in the salty waves breaking gently on rocky ledges below me.

In my opinion, the little blue is a graceful bird, not so serpentine as the tricolored, perhaps, but much more fluid in action than the snowy egret. In fact, its greater grace will distinguish it from a snowy, even at a distance. And, unless it finds itself in a school of fish, through which it will run in a frenzy, stabbing the surrounding waters like an overgrown phalarope, the little blue matches grace with dignity, moving about with the stately deliberation of a great blue. Sometimes it will emulate the patience of that bird by standing motionless for long periods, just as an unhurried diner awaits the pleasure of a haughty waiter.

In my experience, the little blue prefers to be alone or, at best, in company of no more than one other of its kind. But it does nest in colonies of up to one hundred birds, sometimes continuing such friendly relations, after nesting, with twenty or so others — the remnants, no doubt, of its tenement mates. The young of all members of the heron tribe face so many dangers that population growth is never rapid. Young little blue herons are vulnerable to alligators and water moccasins.

It is also said to be partial to the company of snowy egrets and tricolored herons when enjoying salt water. I have seen those species near it at such times but not in what I would call close company, be it seaside pools or flats or even the grassy margins of fresh water. It patrols levees in quite solitary fashion, having an inordinate fondness for the crabs that burrow into and weaken such embankments.

Like most herons, the little blue is not a noisy bird but, and again like the other waders, makes most disagreeable sounds when annoyed or disturbed. Quarrels are accompanied by harsh, strident screams; a hoarse croak signifies its displeasure when inconvenienced; a rough, rising *gerr-gerr-gerr* is given on occasion; while birds swapping nest duties exchange a *quip-a-quee* that sounds, sometimes, like *tell-you-what*.

Like other herons, the little blue is prone to post-nuptial wanderings, my first being such a character. It has so wandered north to Sudbury, Ontario, the Strait of Belle Isle in Newfoundland, and even to Greenland.

Nest: In colonies; a frail, loose platform of sticks lined with fine twigs; 3 to 15 feet up in bushes or trees; almost invariably over or by fresh water. Eggs: 3-5 (4-5), pale bluish-green, elliptical to subelliptical, smooth, non-glossy. Incubation: 22-23 days, by both sexes. Food: Spiders, crustaceans, insects, fishes, frogs and reptiles.

Little Blue Heron

G. LOW 83—

G. LOW 83 —

Tricolored Heron

Egretta tricolor

Breeds and winters from the southern U.S. south to Brazil.

This southern heron is an inordinately slender one, its slimness accentuated by its long neck, so thin in itself that one expects to be able to follow the downward progress of any morsel of food as far as its shoulders. John James Audubon dubbed it "Lady of the Waters." All writers thereafter dealt more or less extravagantly on its graceful form and singular beauty. But, with my usual lack of perspicuity, I fail to see the elegance they have described.

It is also said to be the most abundant heron in southeast North America. I am tempted to agree but only if one excludes the egrets, which are members of the heron family, and the ibises, storks and spoonbills, all of which belong to the same order. And I have never found its numbers overwhelming those of herons known as great blue, little blue, green-backed or night.

The tricolored, or Louisiana heron, to give it the name by which it was known for more than a century, is a very energetic one, the most active of the family. Not for it standing in agonizing pose for minutes at a time, like the great blue or green-backed. Instead, it never seems to stand still, moving about snakily, sometimes rapidly, but never leisurely. When prey is sighted it may crouch briefly, then dart forward, long rapierlike bill transfixing some unfortunate frog or fish with unerring accuracy. Scarcely stopping to gulp it down, it is off again. Very often the bird's posture when hunting is almost level, head, tail and body parallel to the ground or surface of the water. Very often, too, the rapidity of its movements seems more so because of its twisting and turning with wings partly raised, deluding prey into thinking it is going to zig when its intention is to zag. If edibles persist in remaining concealed, the bird will slow its pace but will then vibrate each foot as it slides along, startling something hidden into frenetic activity.

It is a frequent roosting and nesting companion of the similarly sized little blue heron and snowy egret but, like them, prefers to forage on its own. At the end of the day, when home ties are binding, the birds head for the heronry, sometimes collecting in hundreds before the site is reached. Nearing it they plunge downward at high speed, all side-slipping like a mass of disorganized monoplanes at an air show.

The tricolored is not without plumes, but these are not so numerous as those of the egrets. Neither are they particularly colorful. The species was therefore spared the devasting attention of plume hunters of many years ago, so that its numbers have remained fairly constant, any reduction being traced to loss of habitat. Excepting the reddish egret, it is more a coastal species than any other southern heron, rarely moving far inland even during post-breeding dispersal, although a few strays have been recorded from the interior of the United States and, in recent years, along the north shores of Lakes Erie and Ontario in Canada.

Vocally, the tricolored ranks fairly low on the heron musical scale. Croaks and groans express various emotions, from love to alarm. It gives a *quaa* like the little blue, but flatter.

Nest: In colonies; of sticks and twigs, lined with grasses; in bushes or trees or, in Texas, in cacti. Eggs: 3-7 (3-4), pale bluish-green, elliptical, smooth, non-glossy. Incubation: About 21 days, by both sexes. Food: Worms, spiders, crustaceans, insects, fishes, frogs, snakes and lizards.

detail:
American Black Duck
page 74

G. LOW 83

Green-backed Heron

Butorides striatus

Breeds in the southwest triangle of Ontario, and in all the U.S. east of the Great Plains. Winters from the southern U.S. south to northern South America.

The green-backed heron was included in this book only after considerable debate. Is it or is it not a marsh bird? The consensus among authors is that it is not, strictly speaking, a bird of the marsh. It does, however, spend considerable time in marsh edges and may even nest in a tree standing within a marsh; but it frequents more commonly the streams, creeks and shorelines of lakes plentifully supplied with stumps and partly submerged debris.

In pursuing the debate, I turned to my notes, where there is a quite descriptive account of my first sight of each species each year. Therein I noted the habitat occupied by the year's first green-backed heron. Forty-one per cent were seen in flight, with only a third of them seen flying over a marsh. Forty-three per cent were seen perched in a tree, sometimes at considerable height, with none of the trees standing in a marsh. Only sixteen per cent were found within a marsh. It would seem, then, to be not truly a marsh bird.

One, or rather, two of the marsh frequenters provided me with one of my favorite stories. In May of 1953, as we were considering a site for our picnic lunch at Point Pelee, following which we would leave for Rondeau Provincial Park, I realized that the green-backed heron had so far escaped the attention of our party of four. "So," I suggested, "if you will let me pick the picnic site, I'll show you a green-backed heron." No dissenting voices were raised, so we repaired to the little height overlooking Pelee's excellent marsh. Before the first half-moon appeared in a sandwich,

a green-backed heron rose from the base of the bank right before us. I accepted the plaudits with my customary immodesty, privately wondering how I could be so infernally lucky. Then we settled down to dividing our time between bird-watching and appeasing famished stomachs. As we began to leave, a second green-backed heron rose from the same spot vacated by the first. Of the several theories presented me I finally selected the most facetious one. The bird had waited patiently for a hand-out, and when it realized none was forthcoming it decided to eat elsewhere.

The two birds, the only ones seen during our two-day stay, had been at the marsh edge, which was a quite firm area fairly free of marsh growth.

In flight, as Roger Tory Peterson's first field guide informed me more than forty years ago, the green-backed heron looks suspiciously like a crow. Its neck, which is not overly long and which is outstretched only when alarmed, when stabbing prey or when getting under way in flight is, of course, pulled back on the shoulders, as all herons carry it when fully airborne. If the bird is not broadside or if lighting is poor, the bill, not especially long anyway, will seem no longer than a crow's, while the dark plumage will seem raven-black. But there is a recognizable difference in the manner of flying, the wing-beats of the heron being slightly faster while the wings are quite arched. A crow's wings are held flatter, while the bird flaps as if there is just one more wing-stroke left in its failing strength.

The longstanding "official" name was "green heron," its present one a very recent innovation bestowed with the intention of separating it, in the vernacular, from the Galapagos green heron. This is its third name in my memory, as it was originally called "little green heron." Still another name frequently given to it is "fly-up-the-creek," a cumbersome one, perhaps, but very descriptive. Streams and creeks, as remarked earlier, are favorite habitats, places where, if your progress is comparatively silent, you will find a green-backed heron in season. Invariably, it will rise with a harsh *skow* and, as the only avenue of escape may be away from you, will proceed up the small watercourse. Parenthetically, it would seem that none of the old-time birders ever walked down a stream, thus forcing the bird to go with the current. When flushed, it may not go far, instead stopping in some tree from which it will watch apprehensively, twitching its tail somewhat in the manner of a hermit thrush.

While this heron has been known to nest in colonies, the almost invariable rule is solitary nesting; and, just as invariably, solitary feeding. The one exception I have noted occurs in the month of August and in early September, after young are awing and before the southbound migration thins the ranks. At that time, if there is a body of shallow water with its shoreline broken with grounded logs and other erstwhile flotsam, green-backed herons will be unusually numerous, which is to say, one every hundred yards or so.

Nest: A structure of sticks and twigs in bushes or trees, sometimes at considerable height, occasionally on a muskrat house. Eggs: 1-9 (4-5), pale greenish, elliptical to subelliptical, smooth. Single-brooded. Incubation: 20 days, by both sexes. Food: Worms, mollusks, spiders, crustaceans, fishes, frogs, snakes and small mammals.

Black-crowned Night-Heron

Black-crowned Night-Heron

Nycticorax nycticorax

Breeds from a little north of the U.S. southward; and in about the same latitudes in the Old World. In North America, winters from the southern U.S. southward.

Misidentification is not unknown in the birding fraternity. I have had my share of errors — some quite recently and therefore late in my birding life. Roger Tory Peterson, in his *Wings Over America*, gives a dandy involving a blue-colored bottle, to which I can add a railroad-switch stand a friend and I took for a goose standing at stiff attention!

The black-crowned night-heron, near the upper limit of its range at my home and therefore subject to the fluctuations prevalent in wildlife when at range borders, was unknown to me until my fourth year of bird study because it was far from a common species. Then, one September day, I saw a "bittern" fly out from woods to a river. I shook off the impression that the bird had started from a tree, deciding it was an optical illusion, the bird more likely having risen from a marsh or bog to reach treetop level about the time my roving eyes picked it up. A moment later, a "gull" flew from a tree, and this time I was certain it was no illusion, as I could see the bough bouncing. Next, after a few more steps taken in wonderment at these revelations, I found myself under the baleful scrutiny of orange-yellow eyes staring out from a streaked brown bird perched on a limb. "Red-shouldered hawk," I murmured, and cautiously raised my glasses. Once in focus, "bittern," "gull" and "hawk" were quickly discarded in favor of black-crowned night-heron. The "hawk" and "bittern" were birds of the year; the "gull" a full adult.

This species is one of the seven kinds of night-herons found throughout the world, the black-crown having the company of at least one other night-heron everywhere except in the northern segment of its range. What possessed these seven species to concentrate on night fishing is anybody's guess. The habit probably evolved from the extension of the hunting period of an early kind of heron, its descendants persisting, like human fishermen, in trying one more cast before heading home.

The night-heron takes over piscatorial activities at dusk, when more respectable herons are just knocking off for the day. Usually he works the early part of the night shift and the latter part of the graveyard shift, but hunger or the clamoring of young might provoke one into working the clock around. If at all possible, it will roost by day, selecting a well-foliaged tree perhaps some distance from its feeding grounds. When the shades of night begin their descent, the heron takes off. As "gregarious" is their middle name (certainly not "sociable," with all the squabbling they engage in among themselves), a twilight flight will see small groups of three or four headed creek- or marshward. Large groups may adopt a V- or line-formation. If you are near their line of flight but fail to see them, you will certainly hear their flat, throaty *quok* coming down from the inky sky.

Rights to a fishing area are held sacred, the small territory having been won after considerable wrangling. There the bird will stand motionless, head and neck retracted in a characteristic pose, but ever alert for the flash of a fish. If frogs or crayfish are on its menu of the moment, it will stalk with the same cautious tread of a great blue. The ruby-red eyes of an adult, by the way, indicate its ability to see at night.

And by day they come close to threading

needles. I recall being close to an immature one August day. It was standing in a creek that ran through a marsh, but was taken so unawares it took immediate flight — right through a large culvert under a railway! And that requires good sight.

Having read the foregoing you may despair of ever getting a good view of a night-heron. But if you live near the sea you will find the birds regulate their feeding by the tide, heading seaward at the ebb. If you live inland, cloudy days have the same effect on night-herons as they do on nighthawks, both species being moderately active at such times. Further, reviewing my notes, I would say 50 per cent of my observations have been made with the sun above the horizon.

All members of the heron tribe are colonial in nesting habits, with the night-heron preeminently so. And while none of the species earns many marks for tidiness or cleanliness, the extremely slovenly habits of the black-crown turns its nest area into the slums district of the bird world.

Nest: A rude platform of sticks and twigs, lined with finer twigs and grass; placed on the ground in reeds or in bushes or trees, as high as 150 feet up. Eggs: 3-5, pale bluish-green, elliptical to subelliptical, smooth, non-glossy. Single-brooded usually. Incubation: 23-25 days, by both sexes. Food: Crustaceans, insects, fishes of no commercial value, frogs, snakes, young birds and small mammals.

Yellow-crowned Night-Heron
Nycticorax violaceus

Breeds and winters from the southern U.S. south to Brazil.

It was precisely the middle of May. Overhead was a morning sky of bright blue. Ahead of us was a day of studying the inhabitants of the salt marsh by Stone Harbor, New Jersey, unhampered by clouds, unhindered by squalls, and quite devoid of the mosquitoes that would come later. Already the white forms of great and snowy egrets stood out like newly laundered shirts so recently fallen from the line, not a mud spot marking them as yet. The snowys glistened and sparkled, every feather seemingly crystal-glazed. The great egrets were truly white, not exactly a flat white, but without the gloss of their diminutives. Night-herons were as far from our minds as jaegers, so bright was the morn. Then, two birds standing in an open spot of the marsh claimed our attention. Night-herons! And quite oblivious of the time of day, the bright sun and the fact that their eyes are, because of their construction, supposed to be more adapted to use when the sun is obscured, either by cloud or the earth.

Stocky, yet slimmer than a black-crown; a stooped, round-shouldered posture like it but less so in either case; and with a bill thicker and a head larger: all manners of degree not very helpful to one unfamiliar with any kind of night-heron. We were well-acquainted with the black-crown and had a better than nodding familiarity with the yellow-crown. But none of the characters separating the two was necessary for identification today. The morning sun was shining on upperparts streaked with blackish and grayish, quite different from the solid black back of the black-crown. And, with glasses, the more striking head markings were readily apparent.

The yellow-crowned night-heron strikes me as a bird that, a millenium or two ago, was preeminently a salt-water one, feeding not only in salt and brackish marshes by the ocean, but even on tidal flats. In Central and South America and in the Caribbean it continues to restrict its feeding to such areas, but in North America, over a long period of time, it has expanded its distribution to include the Mississippi drainage halfway to Canada, while regular post-breeding wandering has taken it halfway there again.

The yellow-crown seems to be equally at home in a crowd or far from the maddening throng. The latter seems to be the case as one approaches the periphery of its range. In the southeast, colonies, even crowded ones, often with black-crowns for company, are the usual state of home affairs.

Both species share a flat *quok* call but the yellow-crown's is slightly higher and less throaty. This species is more inclined to *quok* in series, a good but not infallible indicator of the species when field marks cannot be seen in failing light. Birds in silent flight may be distinguished from the black-crown by the silhouette alone, the yellow-crown showing a greater amount of leg protruding beyond the tail.

You may properly deduce that, even in less-than-optimum light and at a distance where color is not discernible, distinguishing the two night-herons is a feat by no means impossible, provided you are already acquainted with one of them. Long experience has told me that when any new species of bird comes under the scrutiny of a birder, some subtle difference in form, posture or action will alert the observer that he has in view a kind of bird hitherto unknown to him. Thus, when you are confronted with the brown, spotted young of a night-heron, that feeling will come to your aid if the bird is of the species new to you. You will be aware of something, indescribable at first but leading you to note the bill/leg difference, or that the spotting on the upperparts of the yellow-crown is much less coarse.

Nest: Usually in colonies; a well-built structure of sticks lined with rootlets and twigs; in trees or bushes, at varying heights. Eggs: 3-8 (4-5), pale bluish-green, nearly elliptical, smooth, non-glossy. Incubation: Unknown, but by both sexes. Food: Mollusks, crustaceans, insects, fishes (rarely) and frogs.

G. LOW 83-

White Ibis

Eudocimus albus

Breeds and winters from the southern U.S. south to central South America.

Although the snow bunting is not listed as a bird of Texas, the sanderling is, wintering along the Gulf coast. What, then, was a flock of one of those two species doing at Laredo in summer? Some distance away (an incredible distance, as we later discovered), a flock of apparently one of those species was wheeling and circling, showing white, then dark, then white again as the upper surface of their bodies heliographed cryptic messages to our distant eyes. To reach them and satisfy our curiosity we did more than flirt with the speed limit; we made outrageous advances. But it still took some time to catch up with the birds, some fifty white ibises whose wheeling forms took a final revolution and disappeared in the valley of the Rio Grande. White ibises mistaken for the sparrow-sized sanderling or snow bunting? I can only attribute the error to the unsullied atmosphere of Texas; the birds were seen at such a distance that their size seemed that of sparrows, and the alternating white and dark was reminiscent, to us northern-ers, of small shorebirds as they changed the plane of their bodies in cohesive flight.

At a reasonably close range, one cannot mistake a white ibis for what it is. There is a resemblance to the larger wood stork, whose wing tips are much more broadly black; and as wood storks are fond of circling and soaring high in the air, an error is easily committed. But wood storks take to wheeling only in small numbers, their unsynchronized gyrations suggesting white vultures. White ibises strive for the massed effect. (The use of the plural is preferred, as the species is highly gregarious.)

It is remarkable, too, how a flock, which might consist of hundreds of birds, can materialize so suddenly. One moment the sky will hold only isolated bird forms: a heron here, a fish crow there; a vulture in one sector, a hawk in another. Then, so far above the horizon that you suspect Merlin had a hand in it, will be a flock of the birds, extended neck and legs visible if you are not too distant. If you are closer still, your impression may be that every bird in the flock stopped a fistful of knuckles; a bloodied nose surrounds the base of the bill.

Look away for a moment and the flock will have disappeared. Such was the effect when I first visited Greynolds Park, near Miami, Florida. In this case I think something sent them up from their colonial home on the far side of some growth; but I never saw them rise from there, nor did I witness their subsequent descent. The sequence was very simple: They weren't, they were, they weren't.

I can only assume that their rapid disappear-ance takes the same course as on their evening return from their feeding grounds: long, waver-ing, undulating lines of white that suddenly change to a swirling cloud caught in the vortex of a whirlpool. In just a moment, it seems, the birds have disappeared, like swifts down a chimney.

But where swifts are converging into a small target, descending ibises are obliged to spread out somewhat in order to find roosting space in the tree or trees of their choice.

I saw an uneasy flock go up from the far side of a Georgia pond, taking a few wood storks with it, cruise above the pond in one or two circles (perhaps to ascertain my intentions, although I doubt that I had disturbed them), then drop to two or three trees. I knew for sure that I was in the cotton belt because on the far side of the pond were now three trees liberally gone to seed. They truly deserved the name "cottonwood," so little green was showing.

In Georgia, too, I noticed a wood stork or two in constant attendance. Elsewhere they are the preferred company of other herons, notably snowy egrets. When they all seek the air, though, the ibises dissociate themselves from all other species. A wood stork is usually too thick-skinned to take the hint.

The white ibis is a relative of the sacred ibis, long deified by the Egyptians. And, to the discomfiture of "listers," there may come a time in the not-too-distant future when authorities will be convinced that the white ibis is but a color phase of the gorgeous scarlet ibis, thus reducing their lifelist by one.

Nest: In large, closely crowded colonies; a carelessly made platform of sticks and twigs lined with leaves; on the ground in the west, in reed tangles, bushes or low trees in the east. Eggs: 3-5 (3-4), greenish-white, blotched and spotted browns, subelliptical, smooth, non-glossy. Single-brooded. Incubation: 21-22 days, by both sexes. Food: Crustaceans; insects, small fishes, frogs, small snakes.

White Ibis

Glossy Ibis

Plegadis falcinellus

Breeds and winters from the southern U.S. south to central South America and the Caribbean; and in the Old World, from the latitude of the Mediterranean Sea southward.

Before the early worms had to worry about robins, I was driving to the expansive marsh at Stone Harbor, New Jersey. Silhouettes, then, became an integral part of identification in the first half-hour or so. One bird was particularly intriguing. Its heronlike movements were at variance to the barely distinguishable long, decurved bill, a bill very like that of the many whimbrel around. Then, as the twilight yielded to the first faint flush of the sun, I realized why I had been unable to see color. The bird was a glossy ibis that, notwithstanding the iridescence of its plumage, seems jet black in certain lights.

The eastern coast of the United States is full of bird surprises. In winter, one may encounter North Atlantic gannets as far south as Florida. And in summer, all manner of tropical and subtropical birds move up the coastal plain as far north as the broad marshes of New Jersey. The glossy ibis is one of them. It may be added, for the benefit of northerners or easterners, that if you wish to see birds ordinarily attributed to Florida yet do not relish the trip there, you can do very well by visiting the coastal areas of New Jersey. Such a statement will not find favor with travel agents, of course.

The glossy ibis is about the same size as a little blue heron; but that heron, although it does not sweep the air in the majestic fashion of the great blue, does fly with a certain regality. In my first meeting with a glossy ibis I was astounded by the quick wing-beats, so different are they from a heron's, and so unexpected in a bird of that size. If a lengthy period occurs between sightings I always have difficulty remembering that peculiarity, and aerial identification comes tardily.

In addition, the birds I have seen have been more active on the ground than herons. Their hunting pace seems to be somewhere between the slow stealth of a great blue and the frenzied chase of a snowy egret when that bird is at its most energetic self. If the ibis does find a good food counter, it may halt its impetuosity for a few moments in order to probe a crayfish hole. Its posture while hunting is rather crouched, or at least with the body nearly horizontal but still leaving the strongly decurved bill at such an angle that the tip is always ready to snatch up a water moccasin or a grasshopper.

It is far from a talkative bird, with nasal grunts and throaty sounds constituting its limited vocabulary.

Neither is it particularly sociable, although I have seen no display of animosity to other large waders. It flies to and from feeding grounds in flocks of its own kind, but is not as gregarious as the white ibis. I think four or five represent the most I have seen in flight at one time.

As nests are on the ground in a marsh, the species may be considered colonial, with several to many pairs using the same marshland. But there is none of the crowding associated with the white ibis or some of the herons.

Like certain other birds of this order, the species is seen throughout the tropical and subtropical regions of the world, although a strange discontinuity in the western hemisphere

G. LOW 83—

may be because of its dislike for tropical rain forests. Post-nesting wandering has taken it regularly into many areas in the temperate regions, with strange occurrences in most unlikely parts of the world.

Nest: Usually on the ground in marshes, but also in bushes and small trees; of sticks and twigs, lined with marsh grass. Eggs: 3-4, pale greenish, elliptical to subelliptical, smooth, slightly glossy. Incubation: 21 days, by both sexes. Food: Worms, crustaceans, insects, snakes.

Canada Goose

Branta canadensis

Breeds from Alaska and the Canadian Arctic south to the northern U.S. Winters from the Great Lakes south to Mexico. Introductions have expanded its range almost worldwide.

Present-day birders will elevate bewildered eyebrows when they learn that I did not see my first Canada goose until I had been studying birds for six days short of three years and seven months! Nor had I seen one in those two dozen years or so before recording bird observations became my way of life. For, unless they live far from water in, say, the more arid parts of Arizona or on the edge of the Gobi desert, or in some region equally ignorant of rainfall, present-day birders have as much chance of missing a Canada goose as the Audubon Society has of conducting a Christmas Bird Census on Venus.

During this lengthy period of ignorance, I was resident of Toronto, Ontario, where, according to one historian of ornithology, the bird had formerly (before 1913, that is) been common. I imagine its status during the next two decades was "regular transient, not common." And, as observant as I was, I was apparently never at hand when one of those rare flocks deigned to fly over. But one fateful day an enterprising parks department of some municipality in northeastern North America decided to liberate a few hand-raised birds as an added parks attraction. The surprise now is in finding a stretch of open water devoid of Canada geese.

The Canada goose, which looks as though its long neck is encased in a black stocking with a hole in the instep, is our most distinctive goose. It is further distinguished in being, at the same time, our largest goose as well as our smallest — if, in the case of the latter, one dismisses a

one-inch differential. This extreme variation in size is the result of isolation in past millenia, when various populations increased (or decreased?) body dimensions while still retaining almost all characteristics of the original. Ten subspecies — which is to say, species in the making — have been recognized by taxonomists; these vary in size and shading, the latter running from ashy gray to grayish-brown below, a subtle distinction difficult to detect unless differently colored birds are in the same flock.

While an untrained eye may miss the nuances of underbody coloration of the larger forms, one must be deaf as well as blind to ignore the two smallest varieties, which some authorities consider to be one distinct species in themselves. (Indeed, a few think them two distinct kinds.) One reason for such theorizing is that rather than announce their passage with the resonant *ong, ong* familiar even to non-birders and non-hunters, they cackle and cluck like barnyard biddies and seem as energetic and excitable as house wrens. That was my impression one day when an individual of the "cackling goose" race did its best to upset the serenity of a flock of "giant Canadas" by running about with lowered head, yelping a high-pitched note usually written as *luk-luk-luk-luk*.

Mention of the "giant Canada goose" introduces another facet of this fascinating bird. At one time, a veritably huge Canada goose nested in the prairie region straddling the United States-Canada border and eastward into the Ontario counties bordering Lake Erie. Pale of coloration, as prairie birds tend to be, this majestic bird tipped the scales at twelve to eighteen and even twenty pounds, easily outweighing its next largest cousins, whose maximum was ten pounds. But,

Canada Goose

this large form, naturally very popular with gunners, was sought so much it became an increasingly smaller component of bags until, by 1930, it was deemed extinct. Then, in January, 1962, Dr. Harold Hanson and his crew, weighing examples of large Canadas taken from a flock wintering at Rochester, Minnesota, were at first inclined to believe their scales were faulty. Reassured, they realized that they had rediscovered *Branta canadensis maximus*, the giant Canada goose. Further investigation revealed that far from having sought refuge in some wilderness region, the giant form had blithely continued its existence in game farms, where it nested far more successfully than other strains of the breed. Escapes and deliberate releasing have resulted in such overwhelming numbers of giant Canada geese in the lower Great Lakes region that air-lifts have been used to induce migration, a fact of life ignored by the birds. Why go to such extremes when a popular pastime of humans is "feeding the ducks" summer and winter? So, swelled by progeny raised safely within the boundaries of the most populous cities, the numbers of Canada geese increased by leaps and bounds until, in my daily lists, the species equals the ubiquitous mallard, another interloper which, also through introduction, has displaced the once numerous black duck of the east.

Indeed, a truly wild Canada goose chase can be taken only well north of the United States. There, in the more northern parts of Canada, these wary, sagacious birds still carry on as of old, posting sentries about feeding flocks, a precautionary measure disdained by park habitués. And there, on nests ranging from scanty to bulky down-lined mounds of vegetation, the wild goose will lay its set of a half-dozen eggs or so, flattening herself fully stretched on your approach, confident that her lifelong mate will appear from nowhere and threaten you with wildly flailing wings. Unless you are adept in the ring, it is wise to examine nests only at telescopic range, as an angry gander can administer bone-breaking blows.

In all probability, it will be birds such as those of the far north that you will see flying high, spring and fall, now a wavering skein, now a well-formed V, now an irregular line, but still headed by some trustworthy gander whose suspicion is easily aroused. Their sonorous, clangorous honking is heard from afar, heralding alike the approach of winter and the coming of spring.

It was such a flock I saw and chased, by car, one April day many years ago, long before giant Canadas had taken over our waterfronts. When the birds first appeared over my home, I sensed weariness in their flight and wondered how long they had been winging northward that day. Over the outskirts of Toronto they labored, I in my car threading roads below them, a feat quite impossible today, thanks to the growth of traffic. Fields of stubble, now grown with a great variety of edifices of man's creation, called the birds down. They circled, rose, circled again, and yet again, fatigue etched in every wing-beat. Then, satisfied that the broad field harbored no danger, they settled down, gabbling contentedly, to rest and graze in peace.

Nest: In a depression on the ground, occasionally in trees in old nests of large birds; of sticks, reeds and grasses, lined with soft gray down. Eggs: 4-10 (5-6), creamy white. Incubation: 28-30 days, by the female alone, the male in close attendance. Food: Grasses, grains, sedges, mollusks, crustaceans, and insects and their larvae.

Green-winged Teal
Anas crecca

Breeds from near the tundra south to the northern U.S. and the Mediterranean Sea. Winters from south of the Great Lakes to Central America and the West Indies; and from the Mediterranean Sea south to the Indian Ocean.

Essentially a bird of the marsh and of quiet, reedy waters, the diminutive green-winged teal, which ranks with the bufflehead as our smallest duck, is not averse to wandering in uplands, whether to nest or to feed. I arrived home late one fall afternoon to listen, in open-mouthed amazement, to my wife's account of a drake green-wing that spent an hour or so on our back lawn, feeding on I don't know what, but certainly not on grain fallen from the feeder kept on the opposite side of the garden. The nearest water, a small river that divides two adjoining cities, is a mile distant!

The teal is quite at home in three elements, sometimes completing its overland traveling on foot, tripping along in dainty fashion far removed from the absurd waddle of some of its more distant relatives. In the air, where its small size and quick getaway create the illusion of terrific speed (actually, only about fifty miles per hour), its tightly massed, sometimes large flocks perform intricate maneuvers as adroitly as any flock of shorebirds; and, like them, their erratic course seems to be determined by no apparent leader. Whether in such aerial display or in straightaway flight, their wings whistle reedily.

Afoot, too, it is singularly like a shorebird. One cold January day — the green-wing is hardier than most pond ducks — I watched one walking about snow-covered ground, the bird, in form and action, resembling a rather plump dunlin. On water, it is not as graceful as some

other ducks but still conveys a suggestion of daintiness, induced, perhaps, by its small size.

It may not be true to say it is completely at home in all three elements because it is not an habitual diver, diving as a last resort in the face of certain danger or when wounded, at which time it will hang onto submerged vegetation rather than resurface. Sometimes it clings beyond all recall. In most instances, it seeks safety in the air, leaping into vertical flight, then leveling off into a tortuous course that demands the utmost from gunners. When feeding on aquatic plants it tips up like the larger mallard.

Not unlike many pond ducks, it is most active in the gloaming, which explains the reason for the early start of duck hunters, who rate its flesh so highly when taken in the east. In the west it is at times a far different story. Teal join the bears during or, perhaps more precisely, at the end of salmon runs, when they greatly relish the rotting flesh of spent fish and the maggots their carcasses attract. The odor and taste of putrefaction permeate the flesh of an erstwhile exquisite creature whose gluttony outweighs fastidiousness. When sated with its favorite food of the moment, it likes to loaf, sun and preen on some convenient mud flat or bar.

It is just as catholic in its taste for nesting as it is for food and feeding areas, choosing from islands, through the edge of almost any quiet water (including a roadside ditch) to a dry, upland pasture. The concealment of grass or the shelter of a low shrub is sought almost invariably; and as a further safeguard, the duck, on leaving the nest, will cover the eggs with her characteristic down, a rather dark brown with conspicuous white centers. While the duck assumes all responsibility of incubating, she sometimes re-

ceives a modicum of help from her spouse after the young leave the nest, which is almost immediately after hatching.

It is in the spring, when gallants, vying for the honors of an indifferent duck by arching necks and dipping bills into water, become quite musical. Then, more than at any other time, the drake's staccato, high-pitched whistle is followed by a lower, softer *kirrip*, reminiscent of the call of the spring peeper. The duck's response is almost a bark, a thin, high-pitched *gueck*.

The greenie is quite a wanderer. One banded in California was captured at the island of Belle Isle, which guards the mouth of the St. Lawrence River off the northern tip of Newfoundland. European birds, now said to be conspecific with those of America, frequently pop up in eastern portions of this continent. While the females cannot be distinguished in the field, the Eurasian male has a white bar along the top of the closed wing which is replaced in American birds by a shorter vertical one at the front of the wing. Both marks are conspicuous at some distance as is also the yellowish rear end.

Nest: Constructed of grass, weeds and leaves lined with down in a depression on the ground. Eggs: 8-14 (10-12), white or pale buff, elliptical to short elliptical, smooth. Incubation: 21-23 days, by the female alone. Single-brooded. Food: The seeds, stems and leaves of grasses, sedges and aquatic plants; waste grain, acorns, chestnuts, berries, grapes, mollusks, worms, crustaceans, insects, and salmon and their eggs in season.

Green-winged Teal

American Black Duck

Anas rubripes

Breeds from near the Arctic Circle south to the middle of the U.S., east of the 100th meridian. Winters from the lower Great Lakes through the eastern U.S.

In the very early days following my entry into the field study of birds, I found, much to my chagrin, that I could not count on my daily list the American black ducks I saw unless they were outside the thirty-mile radius of the official Toronto Ornithological Region. The authoritative word was that they were not wild birds. I went along with this edict for a while, then unceremoniously scrapped it.

Sometime in the very late nineteen-twenties or early nineteen-thirties, the Toronto Parks Department liberated some hand-raised blacks that took very kindly to the local environment, prospering mightily as they obeyed the Biblical injunction and went forth and multiplied. Although most if not all their nesting was outside enclosures — the birds being no different from the pheasants that, previously, had been similarly hand-reared, released, and always counted as wild birds — the ducks were in an inexplicably different category.

Ludicrous, yes, but particularly so in the periphery of the Toronto region. There, you would see a black fly in or out of the area and would be in a quandary. These anomalies so offended me I soon called every American black duck I saw a wild one. Here follow two incidents, to show that the black duck of this continent can be tame in the wilds, and wild and wary when surrounded by city pavement.

It was in June of 1951 that "Donald," who might have been more appropriately named "Daisy," as, unlike other duck species, the sex of the American black cannot be told outwardly,

appeared at my parents' cottage in Muskoka, Ontario. It took to sleeping on a raft anchored offshore, visiting the beach from time to time to scrounge handouts from occupants of two of the three cottages there. It was especially attached to my mother, waddling after her "like an ungainly puppy," so they said. I have photos of it taking food from her hand and the hand of her neighbor, the pictures illustrating both its freedom from fear as well as from want, and the fact that it was an American black duck. Unfortunately, it was an absentee on my two brief visits that year, so that I was never able to investigate further. I surmised it may have been a Toronto "Sunnyside Beach" bird, all of which are still adept in the art of panhandling, that may have been enticed more than one hundred miles north by some wild mate. It may also have been raised locally, and not a really wild bird at all.

In 1952 my offices were on the second floor of a corner building. Its front was on a busy thoroughfare, its side on a residential street which my private office overlooked. The opposite corner was then vacant — a jungle of weeds that ran on a couple of hundred yards to a small creek. One afternoon in late July, I summoned my staff into my room to watch the progress of a wild, wary and proud female American black duck leading her brood of six newly hatched ducklings through those weeds. Unperturbed by the sounds of nearby traffic, the parade continued to the graveled drive of the first house on the street, where the leader stopped to reconnoiter. Deeming it safe, she crossed the drive, entered a flower garden and was lost to view, except on those occasions she would stop, stretch head and neck, and survey her surroundings. Then she would hunch down and make further subflora progress. About now she decided she had misread the map, so commenced a return trip, young still in tow, to recross the drive, reenter the weeds, and head in the direction of the creek, which was where I imagined the parade had grouped. The little drama was enacted only eight miles from the core of Toronto and, to office workers, proved as welcome a diversion as a coffee break.

The Toronto Parks Department released mallards at the same time they had the American blacks, other eastern parks and conservation bodies getting into the act about the same period. The wild mallard had previously been seen but rarely in the east, long the stronghold of the American black duck, the latter wilder and warier and a supreme test for the marksman. But soon the mallard gained the ascendancy, either in a pure strain or in hybrid form, as it and the American black duck are so closely related they might easily be accepted as a single species.

The mallard, whether through those releases or not, now greatly outnumbers the American black duck in eastern North America; but the American black, if met in a section of true wilderness, is still as wild and as wary as it ever was.

The habits of the two species are almost identical, although wild American blacks may take to nocturnal feeding, spending the days on water well out from shore, a trait developed in the days of early persecution.

Nest: A cup of grasses, leaves and weeds lined with down and feathers; on the ground, usually near water. Eggs: 6-12 (8-10), greenish-buff. Single-brooded. Incubation: 26-28 days, by the female alone. Food: Grasses, seeds, roots and foliage of aquatic plants, mussels, crustaceans and small fishes.

American Black Duck

Mallard

Mallard

Anas platyrhynchos

Breeds from the Arctic Circle south to the middle of the U.S., and in the equivalent latitudes of the Old World. In North America winters south to Mexico. Introductions have been made almost all over the world.

Two of the many species of the world's birds set out to conquer the globe. One, the cattle egret, is close to achieving its objective. The other, the subject of this sketch, came close to ultimate achievement long before recorded history. But where the egret's *fait accompli* was the result of its own efforts, the mallard, in its final stages, had help from man. As a truly wild bird it breeds from the Arctic Circle to, roughly, the Tropic of Cancer, with some birds wintering south of the Equator. But, like a puppy, the mallard has followed man, either as part of his household or through introductions, almost everywhere. Visit park ponds in almost any country and one of the first birds seen, and usually the first to cadge a handout, will be the ubiquitous mallard.

This intimate association of man and duck goes back centuries, for just as the jungle fowl was the first land bird to be propagated, the mallard was the first with aquatic affiliations. The varieties of chickens developed by man greatly outnumber those of ducks and are of sometimes such bizarre forms as to have lost all identity with the ancestral jungle fowl. But every male barnyard duck carries one characteristic of the wild male mallard — feathers (the tail coverts) that curl above the tail proper. This "duck tail" will be seen whether the birds are the Rouen type, a very obese mallard; gray call ducks, which retain much of the original color pattern; crested white, whose only relief from white feathering is a rough topknot; or the all-white Peking, the bird developed so extensive-

ly in China and which, through its flesh and feathers, plays such an important role in that country's economy.

The mallard may also be the ancestor of all our ducks, wild or cultivated, as it hybridizes so freely with others. The most frequent interbreeding is with the American black duck which, male or female, looks like a dark brown female mallard. But illicit alliances have been made with the pintail, gadwall, wigeon, green-winged teal, wood duck, muscovy and the gray duck of Australia. I have seen a large female mallard with the thick neck of a gray goose, an indication that it is not even faithful to its subfamily, the dabbling ducks; and any day I expect to see one with a white chin strap as, not so long ago, I saw a motley male mallard presumably enamored of a Canada goose.

Males of such crosses continue to flaunt the curled tail coverts, and both sexes usually show the mallard speculum. In nature, hybrid forms are usually but not invariably infertile, the mule (horse *x* ass) being a good example. But the crossing of a mallard and an American black duck seems to have no effect on fertility. A common phase of this hybridization is colored like a black duck with a white chest, a mark that may be the male mallard's ruddy breast trying to reassert itself.

Forty-five years ago and more the American black duck ruled supreme in eastern North America, the mallard being confined, on this continent, to the prairie regions. Then, parks bodies, the forerunners of today's conservation authorities, began releasing hand-raised mallards about the major eastern cities. The ratio climbed from one mallard to ten blacks until equal status was reached perhaps twenty years ago. The black is now very much in the minority. One reason for the mallard's superiority in numbers is that hand-raised birds show no inclination to go wild, seeming to prefer the dependent life imposed on them by propagationists.

The truly wild mallard is a very different bird from the one taking bread from the hand of a park visitor. It is, of course, still an aquatic bird, frequenting shallow waters ranging from large, usually reed-grown lakes to slow-moving watercourses. The prairie sloughs suit it admirably, but swamps in the east are not ignored, although it is preeminently a bird of the open marsh. Be not surprised, however, if you find a nest in a scrubby pasture or uplands some distance from water, a situation leading to high mortality of ducklings when the parent leads her brood to an aquatic element. Irrigated and flooded lands are found attractive while, in winter, sheltered coasts and brackish estuaries are havens. In fall, flocks fly into stubble fields to feed on fallen grain, usually making the two-way trip in the comparative safety of dusk and dawn. Even then, a pass or two will be made before the flock settles down on land or water.

Autumn is also the season for courtship and pairing, when several males will be seen in hot aerial pursuit of a single female. The male winning the tortuous chase will contrive to get the female on water, swimming around her with outstretched head and neck flat on the surface. Head-bobbing by the male is usually the next step, then by both in unison, culminating in dovelike billing. Such actions may continue all winter until actual mating takes place in the spring, although I have seen copulation in January at Toronto.

The drake mallard is treated scornfully by writers with inclinations to anthropomorphize, as it is generally held that nest-building, incubation and care of the young are tasks never undertaken by the male, who spends summer loafing with others also disinclined to keep house. While I have never seen a male shepherding ducklings, I have seen more than one anxious drake in close attendance when I have been examining nests.

On water the mallard is a dabbler, ducking its head under water for a great variety of foods. If necessary, it will tip up, straining to reach bottom while churning the air with brightly colored feet, its stern pointing to the zenith. But when a succulent weed is beyond reach, it will dive, its clumsy splashing and quick reappearance attesting to its status as a novice, and explaining why it is a bird of the shallows. Strangely, young birds can dive quite well, but this art, practiced to escape danger, is soon lost.

Mallards are rarely found singly, one exception being a duckling I saw skittering after a water bug on a pond it had all to itself. If not found in flocks of their own kind they will be mixed with pintail, lesser scaup and American black ducks. It is so much like the latter in habits that the two may prove, in time, to be conspecific. Only the darker color of the black distinguishes it in flight, the not especially rapid wing-beats of both rarely dropping below the level of the body while head and neck angle slightly upward.

Even their voices are similar, the females giving a series of loud, harsh, descending notes exactly like the *wack-wack-wack* heard in the barnyard. The drake's call is thin and pitched higher, a softer, shorter *quek-quek*. He also has a quiet *weeb*, and both sexes murmur conversationally.

Nest: On the ground but occasionally in a low crotch of a tree, a tree-hollow, an old nest or even a building; of grasses, leaves and reeds lined with down and feathers. Eggs: 7-13 (8-11), greenish-buff, elliptical to subelliptical, smooth, slightly waxy. Incubation: 26-28 days, by the female alone. Single-brooded but feral birds may have two. Food: Grains, seeds and stems of aquatic plants, berries, nuts, insects and fishes.

detail:
Snowy Egret
page 41

Northern Pintail
Anas acuta

Breeds from the tundra south to the middle U.S. and the latitude of the Mediterranean Sea. Winters in the U.S. and Central America and south of the latitude of the Mediterranean.

To become deeply involved with birds means to become involved in their home and family life, although that does not necessarily mean sitting within a blind a few feet from a nest. My only blind on this occasion was a thin cover of shrubbery; nor was there a nest before me as the time of year was late November, long past the breeding season. Yet there, in the shallows of a river, was the family, picnic-bent, just as my own family has been on many occasions. Dad was there, quite resplendent in the full regalia adopted by drake pintails the world over. So was Junior, "Bud," I suppose, to his family. He was full grown, of course, and just like his old man except that he lacked the white neck stripe. Cravats would be adopted later. The subdued brownish dress readily identified Mom, still following the mode in pintail circles by wearing her tail longish and pointed. Negative characters identified Debby, who was just like her mother but much paler generally and almost white on her sides and belly. I felt that any moment Mom and Debby would set the contents of a hamper on a checkered cloth while Dad and Bud engaged in a game of catch. But Pop elected to fish, resting flat on the surface, his head and long neck at right angles to his body while, swanlike, he probed the bottom.

This picnicking family was seen on a grass-bordered stretch of the Humber River, at the edge of Toronto, before that stream was fouled with sewage and other poisonous matter. When cleaner waters flowed down the valley, a few members of all puddle ducks, the pintail among them, dropped in for a short visit each autumn. Like the others, though, pintails are more closely associated with reedy ponds and lakes, with the marshy sloughs of the prairie lands possibly ranking highest in their esteem. In winter, fresh water is sometimes forsaken for sheltered ocean bays.

I cannot recall having seen other pintails lie flat with neck extended at right angles, but I have seen many with stern pointing to the zenith, feet waving frantically to maintain balance, while sievelike bill worked at the depths. Gifted with a neck longer than that of other ducks of comparable body size, the pintail is well aware that the bottom of some waters is accessible to it alone of all the dabblers.

The pintail is a sleek, trim, streamlined duck, graceful afloat and awing. More than one old-time writer wrote of the bird as an avian greyhound, both because of its trim lines and because of its fast flight, although I have seen nothing to indicate its air-speed exceeds that of other ducks. I am obliged to accept the findings of others that it has hit sixty miles per hour, according to the clock. This speed, combined with a zigzag plunge to water, means only the top gunners can sample one of the best table birds.

Just as do the humans who seek it with guns and relish its flesh, so does the pintail revel in displaying its skills. With humming wings, a drake will pursue an equally swift female until she succumbs to exhaustion, desire or just to stop harassment. Sometime during these amatory procedures, the drake will parade his finery, enhanced by his long, pointed tail-feathers which, always held clear of the water, are now elevated to an even greater angle. Counterbalancing this feather exclamation point will be his down-pointed bill.

A courting male is not a poor troubador, either, although his music is quite short of equaling Beethoven's *Moonlight Sonata* or a Victor Herbert love song. It is a low, soft, two-syllabled whistle, very pleasing to hear. The lovesick boy seems desperately striving to bring about an elopement as he mews *trrip, trrip*.

The honeymoon over, the drake loses interest in the concert stage and is content with a chattering *kwa, kwa*, as he flies and a weak, wheezy *gseee* that, coming from marsh waters, sounds as though still one more mudhen is hidden from view. The duck, like most females of the tribe, has a quack, hers being hoarse but subdued. She also has a growling note which is just an old pintail custom with no anthropomorphic connotations. Once nesting is over the drake, like all anatids except the geese and swans, stays far enough from domestic cares to escape her complaining tongue. He does condescend to remain close enough to serve as a guard and has been seen in distraction display when nest and young have been threatened. Like other ducks, the female will practice the distraction tactics frequently, unless an intruder reaches the nest with so little warning that her impulsive reaction results in explosive flight.

The close relationship among our puddle ducks is attested by the ability of the mallard to mate successfully with virtually any of them, giving the bird lister the uneasy feeling that some day all the puddle ducks will be considered one species. The uneasiness will not dissipate when I admit to having seen, at Toronto's Sunnyside Beach over two successive winters, a drake pintail with obvious black duck blood.

Nest: Ill-concealed, in a hollow filled with grass, straw and down, the latter brownish with light centers; in grass or marsh vegetation, often as much as a mile and a half from water. Eggs: 7-10 (7-9), olive-buff or pale olive-green, sub-elliptical to oval. Single-brooded. Incubation: 23-24 days, by the female alone. Food: Seeds of pondweeds, grasses, grains and sedges; wild celery, mollusks, crustaceans, insects.

Blue-winged Teal

Northern Pintail

Blue-winged Teal

Anas discors

Breeds from central Canada south through the U.S. Winters from the southern U.S. south to the West Indies and Brazil.

Except for a certain beauty regardless of sex, the demure little blue-winged teal is singularly without distinction. My field notes of more than forty-five years are but a succession of entries concerning numbers seen and, on occasion, references to early or late dates. Nor are such dates exceptionally out of season, for the blue-wing is not a hardy species, rarely given to winter appearances as far north as the Great Lakes.

True, it does have some marks of distinction, but none of these is unique. The chalky-blue forewing that gives the bird its name is also found in the cinnamon teal, the northern shoveler and the Eurasian garganey, and is in the same location and may, in certain lights, look as white as that in the wing of the two wigeons. A white patch before a black or dark tail, quite conspicuous in swimming birds, is duplicated in the pintail, the American and Eurasian wigeons and the shovelers of North America, Argentina and Australia. The flightless teal of Australia has a similar mark, and so has the ubiquitous male mallard, to a lesser degree. Even the white crescent before the eye of our male blue-wing is a mark of another bird, the Australian shoveler.

The sharing of markings with the world's several shovelers suggests a liaison between them and the teals. Certainly the blue-wing's bill is a small-scale replica of the shoveler's spatulate organ, its disproportionate size always evident when blue-wings mix with green-wings. The blue-wing may have left such marks (or picked them up) on its travels, for it has reached the British Isles on more than a dozen known occa-

sions. It has never settled there, for the garganey usurped the blue-wing's niche ages ago.

The blue-winged teal is preeminently a marsh duck, but it can take wetlands or leave them alone. A reed-bordered sluggish stream, a grassy slough or a small pond liberally sprinkled with lily-pads will serve just as well. Nor is grassy cover a prerequisite, as the bird will surprise you by appearing on swampy, muddy ponds, bogs, lagoons and the waters of protected bays of larger lakes. It seems just as happy in a drainage ditch as in the interior of a huge marsh.

Whatever its choice, a whistle-winged, compactly flying flock will scout the locale very carefully before settling down. Several passes are the rule before the birds are sufficiently assured that the place is danger-free. This highly suspicious nature no doubt originates from centuries of persecution, for nimrods of long ago, whose weapons were perhaps no more than stones picked from the ground, knew the blue-wing as a delicacy. Doubtless it was the ancients who first remarked that while the blue-wing courses the air only in flocks of its own kind, it readily accepts waters if other ducks of any species can be seen on them. A few strategically arranged decoys, these early hunters soon learned, quickly dissipated all suspicion.

In addition to their popularity among epicureans, the blue-wing has always offered a great challenge to the man with a gun. On the wing, whether in the open or threading the trees of a swamp, they twist and turn with the agility of a flock of shorebirds. Indeed, they may drop to shelter in the precipitate manner of a woodcock or snipe. Their small size creates the illusion of terrific speed in the air, but tales of speeds exceeding one hundred miles per hour originated before the days of accurate stopwatches. An exceptionally fast blue-wing might top fifty miles per hour, but thirty is considered good form.

Its speedy, twisting flight is placed much to the fore by courting blue-wings. In early spring, when almost all things realize their own particular kind comes in two sexes, the air over a marsh will be crisscrossed by fast-flying teal, usually two males in frenzied pursuit of a duck which is, quite literally, just leading them on. On the water, a pair will also engage in head-bobbing, a toylike action common to several anatids.

But once the duck commences egg-laying the male loses all interest, preferring the secular seclusion of a males' club to domestic life.

The duck will meanwhile be incubating her clutch in some grassy nest which, whether or not ordinarily concealed, generally will be if she leaves it for any reason; then, if she has time, she will cover the eggs with down. A few hours after the young hatch, the diminutive things — so small they find sticks and pebbles serious road-blocks — are led to the nearest water. Whether in the black-and-yellow down of early waddling age or the mottled, drab plumage of adolescence, they are very adept at concealing themselves when danger threatens. Like grouse and quail, they freeze on command, remaining motionless while their dauntless mother employs all the

wiles she knows to lead the intruder to distant parts. If her deception has been successful, she will rise almost vertically, in the manner of all pond ducks, whether from land or water, and rejoin her brood. This is often much larger than the maximum clutch laid by the species, as all ducks seem to gather orphans as a carcass does maggots. One blue-wing was in charge of forty-two ducklings!

Once on the water the young scurry about picking up small aquatic insects. Later they will upend like adults and grub in the oozy bottom for hidden organisms, straining water and mud through the lamellae of their bills.

The youngs' hearing must be exceptional, for their mother's *quack*, although hoarser than the green-wing's, is still soft and very faint. The drakes whistle a rapid *peep-peep-peep-peep-peep* in flight and also softly list *tseep-tseep-tseep*.

Nest: Basketlike, of dry grasses lined with down; on the ground, usually in a depression, usually near water and usually well-concealed. Eggs: 6-17 (8-13), dull white, elliptical to sub-elliptical, smooth and slightly glossy. Incubation: 22-23 days, by the female alone. Food: Algae; seeds and leaves of pondweeds, grasses, sedges, duckweed, smartweed, water lilies, water milfoil; mollusks, crustaceans and aquatic insects.

Cinnamon Teal

Anas cyanoptera

Breeds from southern British Columbia and the Canadian prairies south to western Mexico. Winters from the lower western states southward. Another population is found in South America.

Latin students with no more than a passing acquaintance with birds will question this duck's English name. The specific, or second part of the Latin tag, means "blue-winged," a bird already discussed. The facts are that this bird is aptly named in both tongues. The drake's body is right out of the cinnamon jar, while both sexes have a powder-blue forewing identical to that in the bird we call "blue-winged teal." So, too, has the northern shoveler, which leads us to the obvious close relationship with shoveler and "blue-winged teal." The markings on wings, face and body are repeated throughout the world's supply of shovelers and teal of this kind.

While body color readily separates the two drake "blue-wings," their respective spouses are distinguished only by characteristics too obscure to be of use to the field student. Positive identification of a female is absolutely certain if she is being squired but a dubious proposition if she is alone. But the differences are quite apparent to the drakes; while hybridization is known, it is very rare. One difference not pursued in field guides is that the cinnamon teal is a very quiet, almost silent bird, the blue-wing being considerably noisier. But as differences of degree are apparent only to experienced observers, identification unfortunately cannot be based on either loquacity or taciturnity.

The relationship of the cinnamon and blue-winged teals is obviously very close, so that parallels in their life histories are not surprising. Like the blue-wing, the cinnamon enjoys shallow,

bayonet-rimmed ponds; but being a westerner, it is more accustomed to tule-bordered waters. Drainage ditches and wet fields are preferred grounds of both birds. Evidence of the alkaline quality of the cinnamon's favorite lakes is seen in the chalky deposits about the shores it frequents.

Not that the cinnamon insists on water for nesting. A hollow in a field will serve as well as a rushbed in a marsh, although the field-born young must find their initial walk a long one. But the duck, often assisted by the drake, makes sure her brood, no matter where hatched, is quickly established in the lush foliage of a pond or marsh, where dangers surface much less frequently than in the open water.

The progress toward a family begins in the spring, when drakes, energetically bobbing heads, cluster about a duck. Acceptance is marked by reciprocal bobbing addressed by the female to only one male. The others are not merely ignored; they are ignominiously driven away by both duck and victorious suitor, a procedure so embarrassing to the losers it is surprising that they find courage to try again elsewhere. But they do, and their persistence, plus the seclusion of the "nursery school," has meant an abundance of cinnamon teal, although market gunners did much damage to the species early in this century.

But this near-annihilation did not destroy our little duck's confiding nature. It continues to regard man with equanimity. I found it especially so in British Columbia's Okanagan Valley where, in June, each pond or slough would have a flotilla of young tagging behind a female. As a drake was usually in the offing, there was no doubt of the species under my scrutiny.

Except for the continuity of a family group through fall, flocks of cinnamon teal are virtually unknown, the species being found singly, in

G. LOW 83 —

pairs or, in spring, as a small group of males closely attending a female. But, whatever the size or composition of the group, they are difficult birds to put to wing. They may fly a few reluctant yards but will soon return to where you first found them. This disregard for man makes a study of their habits an easy matter, one custom being a spring pastime in which the drakes engage in a game of leap-duck, one jumping over another with the abandon of schoolboys.

The first cinnamon teal known to science was taken at the Straits of Magellan in the eighteenth century. The obvious conclusion was that it was a South American species, subsequently substantiated by its discovery in many parts of South America north to Colombia. As the Lewis and Clark expedition of 1804-1806 revealed none in the area they traversed, it was thought that the first to be recorded from North America, a male taken in Louisiana in 1849, was a wayfarer from the continent to the south of us. It would seem now that it had straggled east of the migration route of the North American population, which lives chiefly west of the continent's cordillera. An eastern extension of its summer range on this continent has been evident for some time, especially in the north, so that its present range is taking the form of a square.

A few intriguing questions have yet to be answered about the cinnamon teal. Did Lewis and Clark stop short of its North American range at that time? Why the enormous gap between the North and South American populations? In our winter, when representatives of the two populations are in Colombia, do they mingle in any way? When, if ever, will those of North America become genetically distinct from the others? Did the species originate in North or South America? (More probably the latter. It is not only more widely spread there, but time has allowed a few subspecies to evolve; in North America there is only one.)

The only note attributed to the male is a low, squeaky chatter; and to the duck, a *quack* heard with difficulty. It is not, therefore, raising a hullabaloo about successful colonization.

Nest: Variable, of three kinds: A well-woven basket of grass lined with down, either on the ground in tall grass, fastened to marsh growth, or in a hollow on the ground. Eggs: 7-13 (9-12), buff or whitish, elliptical to oval, smooth and slightly glossy. Single-brooded. Incubation: 24-25 days, by the female alone. Food: Seeds, leaves and stems of grasses, pondweeds, sedges and smartweeds; mollusks and insects.

Northern Shoveler

Anas clypeata

Breeds from near the tundra south to the northern U.S., and in the Old World south to the latitude of the Mediterranean Sea. Winters from the southern U.S. to Central America and the West Indies, and in comparable latitudes in the Old World.

There are some who consider the drake shoveler to be a beautiful bird; but only once have I been inclined to agree. In the company of the rising sun of late April I caught one in a small pool. Nor does the species have a uniform gustatory appeal to humans, some epicureans ranking it high, others low. As my table experience with ducks has been limited to a skimpy meal of lesser scaup, I am scarcely qualified to judge. Its taste, so they say, depends a great deal on its recent meals.

While it leans strongly to vegetable matter, there is something specific in its diet that affects its palatability. The more knowing hunters grant it free passage, preferring other pond ducks whose good flavor is assured. Unfortunately, there are some who bang away regardless, happy that the shoveler decoys well and therefore that its flocks, small though they usually be, will contribute to a heavy bag.

Certainly the species was in dire straits many years ago when hunting laws were much less stringent than they are now. Even yet, the shoveler is by no means abundant in the east. It is, of course, more addicted to the marshy sloughs of the prairie regions; but during a swing through the Canadian midwest in the early summer of 1978, I was forced to conclude its numbers were well below those of almost all other pond ducks. This conclusion, though, was at variance with that reached in February, 1976, when shovelers were found to be quite numerous in southeastern Texas. The fact does remain that the sight of a shoveler in northeastern North America at any time is cause for a certain jubilation.

Such sights are most prevalent when frosty weather is either but a memory or not yet fully contemplated, for the shoveler is far from a hardy species, usually being the last to come north in spring and the first to head southward in fall. In fifty years of bird study, I have seen only two at Toronto in winter, which is about par for the course on salt water as well. They also must vary considerably in temperament, as some regularly reach Hawaii in winter while one once carried on to New Zealand.

In respect of hardiness, the northern shoveler is very like the blue-winged teal, to which it is obviously closely related. Blue wing-coverts adorn both species. In fact, each of the world's four species of shovelers has at least one character of our blue-wing, while many authorities would call the bird a shovel-billed teal.

Setting shovelers apart from all other ducks is, without doubt, that spatulate bill, a proportionately large appendage which causes swimming birds to carry it pointing downward as though too ponderous for comfort. In the air the bill adds so much length to the front end that the wings seem set far back. The resultant silhouette is so characteristic that poor visibility is no deterrent to identification. Even in poor lighting the drake exhibits five contrasting colors below — dark, light, dark, light, dark; a sequence especially evident in flying birds.

The spadelike bill comes in handy when the bird more or less stands on end and grubs in the mucky bottom of a pond. Mud and water are squeezed out the fringed and grooved sides while seeds and small animals are retained and swallowed. A more popular way of feeding is for up to a half-dozen birds to form a line and swim about in eccentric circles, bill, head and neck resting on or just below the surface. The leading bird is short-changed but the following ones benefit from the churning feet of those ahead as they stir up the bottom, bringing a greater variety of food to the top.

The unique bill is not immediately apparent in young birds but does develop so rapidly that a few days after the duck has led her brood to water, the young sport a miniature shovel. This is of little use to the diminutive things which, like other ducks, scurry over the surface after water bugs rather than grubbing in ooze. The drake, as is customary among ducks, will be off somewhere with a gathering of selfish fellows, although he will make a token appearance if nest or young are threatened.

He was a much more concerned individual earlier in the spring when he tried so hard to impress the bird who became the mother of his offspring. Joining one or two other suitors in an aerial chase, he would follow the duck all over the marsh. If he contrived to get her alone on the water, he would jerk his bill upward in an imperious "come here" gesture. Assured compatibility would see the duck bow her head, whereupon the two would swim about, one following the other, bills resting on the surface in such a way that water trickled through. The drake's negligence about the home may be the result of the ease with which the ducks sever marital vows. A *ménage à trois*, and occasionally more, stirs up no moral indignations.

The duck has a feeble version of the *quack* of the female mallard, sometimes giving it in a couplet. Like so many of the duck tribe, the drake sounds off quite differently. His most common note, a kind of recognition or flight call, is a series of low, throaty grunts, *kook, kook, kook*; but it is not clear if the derogatory message is intended for himself or his audience. During his aquatic courtship display he will utter a *wonk, wonk, wonk* in the same deep, guttural tone.

On water the shoveler moves about with little deliberation, losing his lethargy when skimming, either alone or in line, or when a distant water insect is sighted. Likewise, his flight may be slow, labored and even uncertain, becoming swift and tortuous if alarmed or aroused.

Nest: A sheltered depression on the ground, of grass lined with down, not always near water. Eggs: 6-14 (8-13), pale olive-buff to greenish-gray, elliptical to subelliptical, smooth. Incubation: 22-25 days, by the female alone. Food: Algae; the seeds of pondweeds, grass, sedges, duckweed, smartweed and water lilies; the bulbs of wild potatoes; aquatic worms, mollusks, crustaceans, insects and larvae, fishes and frogs.

Northern Shoveler

American Widgeon

Anas americana

Breeds in the Great Plains and west from the tundra south to the central U.S. Winters throughout the U.S. (except New England) to Central America and the West Indies.

Naturalists are forever agonizing over the loss of something or other — a marsh here, a woodland there; a passenger pigeon in one century, a darter in another. In the case of our wigeon it is not the bird itself but its long familiar name. It was in 1957 that the American Ornithologists' Union decided to dispense with the tag long recognized by gunners and birders alike, decreeing that, in future, the bird sharing the original generic name of *Mareca* with only two others, the European wigeon and the Chiloe wigeon, would henceforth be known as the American widgeon. No, that is not a misprint. The "d" has since been discarded presumably because it added nothing to pronunciation. (To drop the "p" in "ptarmigan" would raise havoc with old indices.)

In connection with subsequent name changes, I read not long ago that the AOU favors shorter names, which may account, in part, for the dropped "d" but does little to explain why we no longer write of this bird as "baldpate." A surprising number of individuals, though, still *speak* of it as baldpate and not with a guilty glance to the rear to see if the AOU is eavesdropping!

Baldpate was this duck's name since the first blunderbuss roared its shot into a hapless male that ultimately graced the table of some immigrant somewhere in the New World; and that was more probably in the prairie potholes region than in the east.

Like the other prairie dwellers, the baldpate (widgeon or wigeon, as you prefer) began to appear with increasing frequency on northeast-ern North America's ponds and lakes as soon as the virginal forest fell to the ax. I have this to say in my notes of January 8, 1974: " . . . about the same number of black ducks. All took to the water as I approached. Wigeon may now be year-round residents of Toronto and have greatly increased in numbers since my early birding days of the thirties and forties. I think they have been influenced by the many ducks wintering (and being able to winter) at Toronto plus the nearby nesting localities of Luther and Mountsberg."

A point that should not be overlooked is that the two localities referred to have the marshes and marshy bays which the wigeon and other ducks require for nesting and resting. Also, the wigeon grazes almost as much as geese do, and adapts to terrestrial life much more easily than most other ducks. The recent increase in grassy parklands has helped both this species and Canada geese.

On land, wigeons move about like overly plump pigeons; in the air, flocks twist and turn with the agility of sandpipers; and on the water, they pivot and pick at the surface with a daintiness approximating that of phalaropes. Quite an assemblage of families contained in one bird.

While this is not an infallible guide, distant-floating wigeon can usually be identified by their bow-heavy silhouette — breasts low, tail high, wing-tips aimed at a higher elevation, resembling ten-pounders on a frigate whose stern is a velvety black preceded by a contrasting patch of white. If not too distant, you may be able to see a white streak on the folded wing, a mark that becomes a large white patch on the bird's front edge when airborne. (Note that the gadwall's white patch is at the rear.) And always, the characteristic crown-patch of the males suggests a view of the front row from the bright side of stage lights at

Northern Harrier

the burlesque. Wigeon also have a slightly thicker neck than other dabblers, none of which has wine-colored sides.

The wigeon has more versatility than most ducks as it is a grazer, a gleaner on irrigated land and in stubble fields, a tipper and dabbler in shallow water, a pecker if food dots the surface, and a diver if need be. Its limited success beneath the surface, though, has driven it to the life of a hijacker to obtain the wild celery, pondweed and wigeon-grass that tickles its palate. For that reason you will always find a number of wigeon closely attending canvasbacks, redheads, scaups and coots, all more proficient divers than baldy. When one of that crowd surfaces with a mouthful of the wigeon's delicacy, the hard-earned provender is purloined with the deftness of a pickpocket working the football crowd. There is some thought that the wigeon takes the more-or-less trailing leaves, magnanimously leaving the succulent bulbs for the other — as nice a symbiosis as you'll want.

When coastwise or near large lakes during the hunting season, wigeon will seek the safety of waters far from shore by day, returning to land to satisfy hunger by night. But they have been residing in or at least visiting the east long enough now that they have lost some of their inherent wildness and have become tame parks birds. Even golfers find them additional hazards. But if disturbed, either by the proximity of foursomes or other dangers, the female will give a loud *kaou, kaou,* or a louder and prolonged *qua-awk* which, depending on its expression, can reflect the alarm of the bird in proportion to its anxiety. The male's mellow, musical call is usually written *whew, whew, whew,* but *whew, whew, whu* more truly reflects the drop of one-third in the final note.

Nest: Constructed of grasses, weeds and leaves in a sheltered depression on the ground, not necessarily near water. Eggs: 7-12 (9-11), creamy-white, subelliptical to oval, smooth, slightly glossy. Incubation: 23-25 days, by the female alone. Food: Algae; shoots of pondweeds, grasses, wigeon-grass, grains and wild celery; mollusks, crustaceans and insects.

Northern Harrier

Circus cyaneus

Breeds south of the tree line in both hemispheres; in North America to the southern U.S., and to the latitude of the Himalayas in the Old World. Winters in the U.S. and Central America and from the Mediterranean Sea southward.

The northern harrier can be a confusing species. Although it is the only one of its kind in North America, and although it has a number of unique characteristics — or characters which, when combined with at least one other, set it apart from all other North American hawks — it can, on occasion, be misidentified.

For example, it has the long, somewhat narrow wing of a falcon but with wing-tips rounded rather than pointed. At various angles, you feel certain you are looking at one of the larger falcons, especially the peregrine; but you will miss the strong, decisive wing-beats and wonder why. Once I thought the hawk I saw aloft was a falcon having difficulty because of a very strong wind; but then I realized a falcon could fight such gusts with ease. The white rump of our harrier is a giveaway, of course, but that mark, in conjunction with the slightly rounded wings and its occasional habit of soaring in tight circles, will have you convinced you are watching a rough-legged hawk.

At lower levels, especially when quartering a field or marsh, the dihedral, along with the white rump, will identify a harrier without fail. If the white patch escapes your eye, the shallow V formed by the wings will call a turkey vulture to mind. From my observations in winter, the dihedral seems to be abandoned then, although the habit of crisscrossing a field at low elevation

is not. One September day, with yellowlegs all along a shallow shore, I suddenly spotted still one more white-rumped bird and wondered what kind of yellowlegs I had now. It was our old marsh friend practicing some more deception.

The northern harrier is not without blemishes. It rates high as a destroyer of meadow voles and similar destructive rodents, but also draws the ire of those naturalists who deplore the killing of non-game birds, particularly those with attractive plumage or melodious song. As the harrier seeks ground-dwelling prey, a scarlet tanager, say, is quite safe from it, but grass-haunting sparrows are not necessarily so. I think, though, that when the harrier makes a meal of, say, a savannah sparrow, it is a case of mistaken identity. I know that the actions of a sparrow creeping or running through grass remind me very much of a meadow vole. Doubtless a harrier is similarly misled. A bird of prey, be it hawk or owl, is conditioned to strike interesting movement, and as its taste buds are rather inefficient, its error goes to its stomach undetected.

The small birds themselves, though, may disagree with my theory. I wondered once why grackles, engaged in feeding deep in rushes, flew en masse to neighboring trees. The answer to my query came along shortly — a low-flying, beautiful, gray adult harrier, ready to pounce on anything in motion in the marsh. Extreme hunger may precipitate an attack on a healthy duck, but the waterfowl entering into its diet may have been mortally wounded not long previously.

The northern harrier "quarters" a field or marsh, which is to say, it flies back and forth low over the ground. When so intent on its hunting, it is too busy to indulge in vocal expression. It is only about the nest and when displaying that the chattering call is given, the feminine version of which is the higher and thinner.

In recent years the use of the name "northern harrier" has gradually supplanted the old one of "marsh hawk." Its recent acceptance by the American Ornithologists' Union brings the name of the American race into agreement with the Old World form.

Nest: Constructed of grasses and sticks on the ground or in low shrubs; frequently in a marsh. Eggs: 6-12 (4-6), bluish-white, sometimes blotched brown, rounded oval. Incubation: 21-23 days, by the female alone. Food: Insects, fishes, frogs, lizards, snakes, birds and small mammals.

Clapper Rail
Rallus lonirostris

King Rail
Rallus elegans

Clapper Rail: Breeds and winters in salt marshes on both coasts of North, Central and South America, from the latitude of New England south to Peru and Brazil. King Rail: Breeds in the U.S., east of the Great Plains. Winters in the southern U.S. and Mexico.

Consternation entered the lives of birders on the appearance of S. Dillon Ripley's *Rails of the World*, for therein, in almost unassailable logic, the author lumps together the king and clapper rails. Since that time, birders who have claimed both species have lived apprehensively, awaiting word that the American Ornithologists' Union agrees, thus depriving them of a species possibly earned only after considerable effort. Most happily, both kinds still stand on their own large feet.

In the past, the first criterion for field identification of the two species was the habitat, the salt marsh being the abode of the clapper, the fresh-water marsh being called home by the king. Birds heard in brackish waters were a toss-up, but if they could be seen, the field man fell back on the second criterion. A ruddy bird with strong barring became a king, a grayish one not so evidently barred was a clapper. And the fact that the clapper is a washed-out version of the king is the cornerstone of Ripley's thesis. It was this distinction that fostered the original belief that the clapper was the young of the king, few young birds of any species being as colorful as their parents.

Other facts supported Ripley. The large rails of the southern and western states resemble king rails more than do those of the east, but are grayer at the bend of the wing and have weaker marks on the body. Going farther south to the fresh-water marshes of Mexico, one is confronted with a clapper so tawny some consider it a race of the king. The fresh-water/salt-water rule takes another beating in the lower Colorado River, where one long-established subspecies of the clapper gets along very well in a fresh-water habitat. James Bond stresses the difficulty in separating the king and clapper rails on those Caribbean islands where both are known to occur. Finally, the birds themselves have doubts, for hybridization is not unknown where the two live in close proximity.

At this point in the summary, I am regarding, with some perplexity, a note in my journals which states: "I saw a king rail in a South Carolina marsh which wetland, although within a mile of the broad beaches, had all the fundamentals of the fresh-water variety." Presumably, the AOU will allow the rule of salinity to prevail.

The volubility of the two birds is well known, but their vocabulary as found in literature provides no answer for the separation of king and clapper rails. One reason is because of the failings of the human ear; the other, because the call which was published as that of a king may have been, in reality, coming from a clapper!

The clapper's name originated in its common call, which was said to resemble the clapper of years ago. I think I know, or knew, the noise-maker referred to but cannot quite relate the rapid *cha-cha-cha* repeated up to twenty-five times and which, while becoming lower, increases in time to end in a roll. This is the call that might come from a thousand throats, all startled by one foreign noise. There seems to be two calls associated with conjugalism, one a low, grunting *ump-ump-ump*, the other a harsh *kick-kick-kick*. Females give a catlike *purr* while the general alarm note is a *kek*. But the variety is almost infinite, for each subspecies, and there are many

G. LOW 83—

in the clapper branch, has a regional dialect.

The king varieties are inclined to wander into cultivated stubble and grassy fields in search of grain, at which time they might appear like large, long-billed, big-footed chickens, with a habit of flirting the tail or keeping it cocked to display the white under its tail-coverts. Whether startled in a field or in a marsh, its preferred mode of escape is by running rather than flying. The flight of both species is typically ralline, a weak effort with legs dangling to almost touch vegetation. On migration the flight is stronger, with neck outstretched but with the bird still low to the ground.

Such a terrestrial bird living near water is certain to have ducklike attributes, so, as expected, these rails swim fairly well but at a slow pace, the head bobbing in unison with the feet. They also dive but with still less proficiency. And when seeds are beyond reach, they climb the stalks and haul the seeds earthward.

All and all, interesting characters, the salt-water version of which I never expected to see, it is said to be so secretive. Yet each visit to coastal marshes has produced clapper rails, while countless jaunts to fresh-water marshes have yielded not much more than that *ca-ca-ca*-cophony of protesting birds. None of my salt-water excursions equaled my first, however, when I outdid the great Audubon. I witnessed the copulation of the clapper.

Nest: Sometimes only a grass-lined scrape, but usually a well-made cup of grasses and reeds; on the ground in a marsh, in bushes, or attached to marsh vegetation, from 6 to 18 inches above the water, generally arched in the latter case. Eggs: 6-13 (8-11), pale buff, spotted or blotched with browns and grays, subelliptical, smooth and glossy. Incubation: 20-21 days, by both sexes. Food: Seeds, tubers, roots, waste grain, leeches, mollusks, worms, crustaceans, insects and fish fry.

King Rail

G. LOW 82 - ©

Virginia Rail
Rallus limicola

Breeds from central Canada south to the tip of South America. Winters almost throughout the U.S. south to central America.

Determining the presence of Virginia rails is an easy matter. Simply toss a pebble into a likely marsh, then sit back to catch the clatter of calls. Visual recording is more difficult, requiring any of the three following tactics. You can pole through a cattail jungle and, if fortunate, will be rewarded by the sight of a Virginia rail as it rises and flutters feebly for fifteen yards, dangling legs accentuating its weak effort. Or, you can quietly meander along any of the growing number of marsh boardwalks and surprise a bird slipping from one open spot to another. Or, and this is the way I find most satisfying, you can sit quietly by a marsh in spring, before vegetation is fully grown, and with a little good fortune catch one emerging from the tangle, treading cautiously and deliberately over the ooze, absurd tail flicking with each step.

A sudden movement on your part and the bird will vanish, as if a wraith. It may take feeble flight as aforementioned; it may dash rapidly into and through the trails it knows so well; or it may plunge boldly into the water, if the depth is sufficient, and swim to cover, its bobbing head punctuating each foot stroke. Its most entertaining mode of escape is a trot over lily pads, suggesting a game of aquatic hopscotch.

Quiet, almost stealthy movements are essential to successful Virginia rail watching. I engaged in a lengthy staring contest with one that I caught standing in a watery wagon rut in a wet meadow. The first snaillike movement to raise my binoculars was enough to send it off to set a new wagon-track record.

Rarely seen, even by the most experienced

observers, it is surprising how many will occupy a marsh. The new technique, that of using a tape-recorded song to call up birds, resulted in the discovery that twenty-four rails occupied a marsh of a few acres. This is encouraging, as all rails are so secretive that we have no way of telling how they are combating the relentless decrease of their wet habitats. Nor are the birds visible on migration, as they move by night. Our only evidence of the flight is the discovery of dead and disabled birds that struck objects as low as fences, as the flight is conducted at no great elevation. Yet, weak as is its effort when flushed, it manages to reach and winter in South America.

Elusive as it is, it is the antithesis of the waxwing, whose note is but a hissing lisp. Anyone who has dwelt by a marsh will stress the difficulty of sleeping in early summer, as hour after each of the twenty-four the vociferous male Virginia is in song. The few pauses indulged in by one bird are admirably filled by another. If my ears and the interpretations of other writers are correct, the phonetic rendition of the song is variously spelled *cut-ah* and *kik-queeah*. It is vibrant, staccato and so metallic as to sound like a hammer striking an anvil. The bird usually warms up with a few *cuts* or *kiks* before launching into the disyllabic phrase. I think it is this song that some authors write as *kid-ick, ka-dick, ka-duck, ke-tick*, and *click-ick*, although it does not sound like that to me. A Richard McGeer seems to have entered the circle of its acquaintances comparatively recently, for a new rendition, *Dick, Dick, Dick McGeer*, is now known to be part of the Virginia rail's repertoire. For long this call was attributed to the black rail.

Another frequently given sound, which seems to be an alarm rather than a song, is a series of piglike grunts, given rapidly on a descending scale. This is one of the most peculiar noises coming from a marsh, which is certainly no place for a shoat. Nor is it easy to locate the author. I have stood facing the sound, which seemed to rise from my very feet, yet could not see the bird. The quality of the note is so far-carrying that the pseudo-porker could have been many yards away. I cannot transform this note into the mallardlike *quack* that some do.

In addition to the notes that have some phonetic rendering, the Virginia rail has many indescribable ones. They include squeaks, chirps, moans, chatters, kicking sounds, froglike croaks, henlike clicks, clucks and cackles, and a serene rising whistle. A *kek* means danger, while the female's affirmative response to the male's song is a low *kee* or *kee-ah*, varied with a flickerlike *keeu*. It has more varieties than a pickle manufacturer.

There is some variety in its habits and habitat, too, as it easily climbs reeds and bushes to reach seeds and berries and, in fall, will desert the wetlands for stubble fields and fallen grain. One Virginia rail surprised me by rising from a dry, weedy field a half-mile from water.

Nest: A loosely woven yet compact cup of marsh vegetation lined with cattail blades; on the ground in or at the base of a clump of grass, or attached to such vegetation within a foot of water. It is often covered with a loose canopy. Eggs: 5-14 (6-12), pale buff, sparingly spotted about the larger end with reddish-brown, sub-elliptical, smooth. Incubation: 19-20 days, by both sexes. Food: Seeds of grasses, rushes, wild oats and wild rice; berries; leeches, earthworms, mollusks, crustaceans, insects and larvae, small fishes and frogs.

Sora

Porzana carolina

Breeds from near the tree line in Canada south to all except the most southern states in the U.S. Winters from the southern U.S. south to the West Indies and northern South America.

The rails are such a secretive lot that I expected to see one, in the very early days of my birding activities, only at the expense of crawling through a marsh on my hands and knees. But before my first half-year was up I was gazing, open-mouthed, at not just one, but three, none peering furtively through cattails but as exposed as any domineering crow. Nor were they standing on the oozy ground of some wetlands but were climbing partway up weed stalks in order to pull the seed-laden tips to within reach. All had presumably walked half a mile from the nearest marsh; and all, or their progeny, were watched for four consecutive autumns as they engaged in this unraillike trait at the same place.

That marsh is now no more; nor could the birds find sufficient cover in the valley to complete their walk in safety. Like all other marsh creatures, the sora has suffered through loss of habitat, but it is still North America's most abundant and most widely distributed rail. Although just as secretive as any other, it is seen more often because its numerical superiority increases the probability of its coming into view.

As with the Virginia rail, a pebble tossed into a marsh will induce a cacophony of sora sounds, usually interrogative, henlike *kuks* and *clucks* interspersed with squeals and yells in extravagant variety. In fact, any loud noise will serve to trigger the medley. But its entire vocabulary is given offstage. Just as large an element of luck enters into viewing soras as does seeing Virginia rails, with the best method a passive approach at twilight. Inconspicuousness does not seem to be necessary as they have appeared for me when I have been in a most exposed situation. But their deliberate tread, the jaunty flick of the tail that seems synchronized with the feet, the chickenlike nodding of the head, all vanish on your slightest move, and the bird dashes madly for the friendly cover of cattails, white under tail-coverts flashing an appeal for peace. Keep truce with the sora, though, and it will repay you with confidence, even to feeding in your poultry yard, if you should happen to have one in these days of massed poultry production.

There was a time when the sora had little confidence in man. In the days when market shooting prevailed, hunters poled their way into marshes, starting soras into their loose, feeble flight. As the birds fluttered low over the reeds, grazing the tops with dangling legs, few gunners were unable to fill their bags, and all for a bird so small it took longer to pluck than to eat.

Sora shooting is still conducted in places, with the hunters still being surprised at the complete disappearance of the birds when the first frost strikes the marshes. Overnight, the soras vanish, moving southward in flocks of as many as one hundred, flying now with a stronger, steadier yet still labored flight and, because of their out-stretched legs and neck, looking like diminutive cranes. Like the Virginia rail, they fly at no great height, frequently coming to grief against low structures. Their migration will take some as far as northern South America. There will be stopovers, of course, yet the bird regularly crosses the Gulf of Mexico and the 700-mile watery stretch to Bermuda. It has also made unscheduled landings on vessels far at sea. At least five birds have demonstrated their

endurance awing and successfully reached Great Britain, to exchange greetings with their counterpart there, the spotted crake.

While the sora is a bird of the marsh, it is, like other short-billed rails which, colloquially are called crakes, more a land than a water rail, making greater use of stubble fields and bush-dotted hillsides in fall than does the Virginia. It will sometimes winter in brackish or even wholly salt marshes, but on its travels and for summer living it prefers wet, grassy meadows and fresh-water marshes, where its laterally compressed body can slip through stems with consummate ease. Its versatility is heard in its voice and seen in its actions, for it walks like a chicken, swims like a duck (with appropriate chickenlike motions) and dives like, well, a sora. It walks and runs under water with the ease of a dipper and tries your patience by remaining below the surface as it clings to submergent vegetation with bill and feet.

It introduces still another barnyard character by whinnying like a horse. This series of loud, far-carrying, short and high-pitched whistles descends in pitch, lowers in volume and slows in tempo. It is a spring call, just as is a querulous, plaintive *cur-wee?* that is remindful of the location call of the bobwhite. One of these calls is the song of the male, while the other could be the response by the female. William Brewster claimed the female gives the whinny; Frank M. Chapman that both calls are given in chorus, like an antiphonal duet by male and female. Brewster also claimed it gives a quieter version of the Virginia's *cut-cut-cuttah*, while E. H. Forbush credited the sora with mimicry, imitating flickers, whip-poor-wills, screech owls and bobwhites. As the bird calls from cover, it is difficult to understand how such eminent authorities determined the authorship. One note, a sharp, ringing *keek*, can usually be traced to the sora, which may still be in view when this alarm call is given.

Sora

Nest: A well-constructed, fairly compact, shallow basket, woven of marsh vegetation and fastened to or supported by reed stems as well as usually well hidden within them; sometimes on the ground or on a raised platform. There may be a rounded canopy and an evident runway. Eggs: 5-18 (9-15), buffy, finely and irregularly spotted reddish-brown, subelliptical to oval, smooth, glossy. Large clutches are arranged in the nest in two or three layers. Incubation: 17-19 days, by both sexes. Single-brooded. Food: The seeds and leaves of smartweeds, water millet, wild rice and wild oats; mollusks, worms, crustaceans, insects and small tadpoles.

detail:
American Avocet
page 123

Purple Gallinule

Porphyrula martinica

Breeds in the southern U.S. south to the West Indies and Argentina. Winters from the Gulf states southward.

This bird is usually described with an abundance of adjectival superlatives, all indicating great beauty. True, it does have some appeal with its rather flamboyant mixture of blues and purples, browns and reds, yellows and whites — an assortment and combination of colors found chiefly in the work of interior decorators striving for effect rather than pleasure. The painted bunting of, strangely, much the same range, has a similar effect. My impression of both, an opinion apparently shared by very few others, is an attempt to present the lights of Las Vegas in feathers.

The purple gallinule seems to be a garish version of the common bird. Same size, same form, and much the same habits. It is, though, confined (although not entirely) to the tropical and subtropical regions of the New World. Don't confuse it with the much larger bird of the Old World (India, South Africa and Australasia) called swamp hen in some places, purple gallinule in others.

One wonders how and why the New World bird separated from the almost cosmopolitan common gallinule, which has recently been rechristened the common moorhen. The purple gallinule associates with the other quite freely. Another common associate is the American coot.

In my almost limited experience, the purple species is seen more rarely than the common moorhen, although, like the latter, it is said to be a common bird within its range. I think it may be, because while both species frequent marshes well grown with a variety of marsh plants, the moorhen will spend much more time in the open ponds, channels and waters quite devoid of emergent vegetation. The purple gallinule, on the other hand, tends to keep to cover so dense as to be impenetrable by all except another purple gallinule.

It emits the same henlike cackles as does the moorhen, including the variations so endeared by all members of the rail family. And, because all, including the two gallinules, give vent to notes of alarm or pleasure from deep cover, the uninitiated birder may have no idea what species is making such a racket. The two species do differ slightly in the call given most frequently. The moorhen gives a *kik-kik-kik*, sometimes ad infinitum. The purple doubles the syllable to *kiddy-kiddy-kiddy*, finishing with *kid-up, kid-up, kid-up*. Other calls have been attributed to this species, all resembling more-or-less familiar noises in the world of man; but as all rails have the same ability to startle and confuse us, it is difficult to give many sounds emanating from a marsh a specific origin.

Until you get to know the species, it is best to let strange marsh sounds go unidentified. Wait, then, until you see a rotund neon sign swimming with head jerking like a walking chicken, or striding agilely over the leaves of floating plants, or climbing about bushes, which the purple ascends to the height of a man.

Nest: A mass of marsh vegetation attached to surrounding reeds and rushes. Eggs: 5-10 (6-8), buff, spotted browns and grays, ovate, smooth and with little gloss. Food: Seeds of aquatic plants and cultivated rice; worms, mollusks.

Common Moorhen

Gallinula chloropus

Breeds in southern Ontario and Quebec and throughout the U.S. to the West Indies and Argentina; and from Europe and central Asia southward, except Australia and New Zealand. In the western hemisphere, winters from the southern U.S. to northern South America.

There seems to be something awry with the common moorhen in North America. Beardslee and Mitchell, in their *Birds of the Niagara Frontier Region*, state that its numbers declined markedly in the nineteen-fifties. While that region, like so many others, has experienced some habitat loss, other unknown factors must be involved, as there seems to be an imbalance between loss of marshes and reduction of birds. The findings of these two authors (more properly, the lack of them) are confirmed by my own experience. During the nineteen-thirties and nineteen-forties, I recorded good numbers of moorhens about Toronto, and when the bird seemed to vanish in the fifties, I attributed it to the loss of the excellent marshes in the Humber Valley and at points on Toronto's lakefront. Something more drastic must have happened so that, even now, the sight of a moorhen is, to me, an event.

In undiminished numbers, the same species occurs in England, where its name of moorhen is now applied to our bird, for long known as common or even Florida gallinule. This name is not derived from "moor," that tract of inhospitable land which, with fog, is so popular with British mystery writers, but is a corruption of "mere," a small lake. This would seem to be an ill-chosen name; whether gallinule or moorhen, the bird is not found on lakes of any size unless the edges are well grown with rushes and flags. While moorhens delight in walking about the muck and flattened vegetation of marshes, they do insist on some open water, their habits connecting the more secretive rails and the quite conspicuous and highly aquatic coots.

The North American and English forms differ widely in their acceptance of humans. Not only does the British moorhen abide comfortably on ponds in English parks, it wanders about the neighboring turf with the aplomb of a mallard, adroitly sidestepping human pedestrians. In North America, the moorhen insists on some privacy. Although it may swim about quite openly, it keeps its distance no matter what kind of water it is on.

On land or water, though, the moorhen has all the mannerisms of a barnyard biddy. It certainly nods like one, even when swimming. It has taken the coot's habit of moving its head in unison with each paddle stroke or step and magnified it many times. Once an observer becomes familiar with the head motion of the two birds, identification can be accomplished from afar, so different are the two.

The moorhen reproduces all the sounds of an extensive henyard, adding a few of its own invention. Its various calls are loud, noisy and shrill, frequently discordant, sometimes complaining. Some have been described as trumpetings, while one writer likened one call to a bugle horn! The warning note is a penetrating, froglike *curruk*. A *caak*, given when excited, is shortened to a rapid series of *keks* as excitement rises. Another call is a *ko-ko-ko-ko-ko*, something like that of a pied-billed grebe. The male's song, interspersed with a display of its red shield or a rear picture of its tail coverts which, with its flank markings, then present one large white area, is a harsh *tickut*. One wonders, though, how the race is perpetuated, as the hen ignores both physical and vocal efforts.

The coot has overly large white feet with lobed toes. The moorhen has extra overly large feet, its greenish stockings held in place by a red garter at the top. There is no webbing nor are there lobes, yet the bird swims just as easily as if it had both. The extra-long toes enable it to walk or trot, with a high-stepping gait, over floating marsh vegetation jaçana fashion.

On water, the moorhen floats stern high, feeding much like a chicken on land or a phalarope in mid-ocean, pecking at the surface between pirouettes. Sometimes it will tip up like a puddle duck and is said to dive on occasion. If escape by swimming or flight seems impossible, it resorts to sinking like a grebe until just its bill is exposed. Like the coot, it must patter over water before becoming airborne, its flight initially being weak and labored, with loosely dangling legs. Once under way, it draws its legs up and flies strongly. Most flights we see are short and low, as migration is a nocturnal affair, which led to a not-so-ancient thought that it hibernated! Inability to monitor the moorhen's migration was coupled with its sudden disappearance in fall, the silence following its departure being of a deafening sort. A pond of moorhens is an exceedingly noisy area with, in spring, both vituperative and physical warfare.

Moorhens and coots are well described as lugubrious. One moorhen that fully deserved that description was the only one in view on Toronto's Grenadier Pond many years ago. I watched it swim to and then along the opposite shore until it came to a log jutting out from land. Laboriously, it clambered aboard, oblivious of the dozen or so black ducks snoozing on its surface. There was ample room for several moorhens at the floating end but this finicky one favored a bunk close to shore, so it started a cumbersome course to its objective. With its large feet striking ducks somewhere, usually squarely on the back, it tumbled them into the water one by one, treating me to the first game of duckpins I ever saw. Then, having scored a strike (I suppose, as I was not up to the refinement of the rules), it settled down to await the attention of the pin boy.

Nest: A basketlike platform of reeds, rushes and grass among and usually attached to reeds at or above water level, or on the ground. It is sometimes arched and usually has an entrance on one side. Eggs: 6-13 (7-11), buff, spotted reddish-brown, subelliptical, smooth and glossy. Usually 2-brooded, sometimes 3. Incubation: 19-22 days, by both sexes, with the young of one brood sometimes caring for those of the following one. Food: Leaves and seeds of pondweeds, duckweeds, grasses and berries; worms, mollusks, insects and larvae, and sometimes eggs and chicks of other birds.

Common Moorhen

American Coot

Fulica americana

Breeds from central Canada south to Central America. Winters from the northern U.S. southward.

When a rustic, visiting a zoo, saw a giraffe for the first time, he exclaimed, "There ain't no such animal!" The same disbelief may be expressed when first viewing a coot. As it has feathers, it is obviously a bird, but one with an expression so comical it has given birth to the phrase "silly as a coot."

Structurally, the world's nine species of coots, one of which is suspect, are allied to the rails, perhaps through the less-accomplished gallinules. But, adding to their incongruous appearance, coots have a bill so chickenlike they might be taken for escapees from the henyard were it not for their progress on water, where they move with the ease of a duck. They differ from anatids in one respect, as they swim with a level rather than a curved back. They dive, too, better than a mallard but not so well as, say, a redhead, taking a preparatory leap as though launching from a springboard, and popping up again like a large, black cork. On land they move about somewhat clumsily, the head, bill and hunched back reminiscent of guineafowl. Now, the ungainly size-fourteen feet will be in view, toes lacking the webs of a duck and prompting the query, "How does it swim so well?" A closer examination is usually not invited by the birds, although when protected they will become tame enough to feed from the hand, making themselves unequivocal pests in the bargain. When familiarity is a reality, they will reveal toes with scalloped edges, something like the lobes on a grebe's foot but with three rather than one per toe.

Summing up, a coot is a gallinule-like rail with the bill of a chicken, the form of a guineafowl, the aquatic ability of a duck and the toes of a grebe. What more can one ask in a package?

Vocal variety? It's there, too!

The American coot does have a few select noises it makes during its courting, one being a rhythmic and monotonous *kaa-haa, kaa-haa, kaa-haa*. But after that the variety of sounds exceeds those of a rock band. The terms used by various authors in describing them are: Cackles, cacks, chuckles, clucks, coos, coughs, croaks, grunts, plunks, quacks, squawks, toots, wails and whistles. None of these is musical, some are rough and grating and most are loud, shrill and harsh, although the "coo" is soft and the "plunk" froglike. As their incessant quarreling ceases only during the incubation period and since the birds are very gregarious otherwise, even a flock can best be described in plurality as a cacophony of coots, antithesis of a whisper of snipe.

Coots are undeniably marsh birds, but they favor marshes that have open water toward or in the center, where they are safe from all enemies save large hawks like the bald eagle, or, as I observed in Arizona, the osprey. Sometimes a rush-bordered sluggish river or the quiet waters of a lake off a reed-grown shore will attract them. Most winters I have found one or more in protected harbors on the lower Great Lakes, where they mingle with the ducks cadging from humans. The white bill and the nodding head, moving in unison with each foot-stroke, are conspicuous unless the ducks are tightly packed. Winter is about the only time they spend on brackish or salt water, where they may seek the shelter of marshes or a secluded cove.

Much hardier than moorhens, coots push northward in late winter, deigning to wait the arrival of springlike weather. Hundreds, even thousands, will join pochard and wigeon congregating over beds of wild celery when they exploit the superior diving abilities of canvasbacks by snatching the waterweed from the bill of a resurfacing bird. After nesting, they soon regroup, to bedevil the ducks anew. This is more apt to be the time when huge "rafts" will form offshore, an immense flock that will ball even more compactly on the appearance of some raptorial enemy.

While not entirely reluctant to take wing, they prefer to escape more terrestrial enemies by skulking in marsh grass. If wing-borne escape seems more expedient, the birds spatter across to a distant haven, their rapidly moving feet and wings leaving water craters and a V of coarse spray. When conventional air travel is indicated, they fly strongly and vigorously, at no great height, at which time it is evident their aerial ability is less than that of ducks but superior to that of the moorhen. Migration is possibly easier to them than it is to rails, but not so easy that they scorn walking. Ten thousand passed through one area in four days, all on foot!

Of the countless times I have seen coots on water, on land, occasionally in the air, the most memorable have been those of early summer, when a pair shepherds its bizarrely marked young about the borders of a marsh. The tiny balls of fluff are just as black as their parents, but where the Nubian coloration of Mom and Dad is relieved only by the white bill and the white undertail coverts (which are exposed in nuptial display), the young wear a collar or ruff of orange and yellow threads, with additional filaments scattered on the back.

Nest: Sometimes in large colonies; a firmly woven, bulky cup of marsh vegetation lying atop a platform of the same material, which may be on a bed of reeds or floating on water, anchored to surrounding reeds in the latter case. It is usually well concealed but sometimes quite exposed. Eggs: 7-15 (9-11), light pinkish-buff, uniformly speckled with dark brown and black, subelliptical, smooth and slightly glossy. Incubation: 22-24 days, by both sexes. The male takes charge of the first arrivals while the female continues incubating. Food: Seeds, roots, bulbs, leaves and stems of various plants, especially marsh grass (*chara*) and wild celery; worms, mollusks, crustaceans, insects and larvae; fish spawn and small fish and tadpoles.

Sandhill Crane

Grus canadensis

Breeds in the tundra of Siberia, Alaska and Canada west of Hudson Bay; in the Great Plains of the U.S.; and in Florida. Winters in the southern states of the U.S.

Tiny Marsh lies in Ontario about midway between the City of Barrie and Georgian Bay of Lake Huron. It is not tiny (it gets its name from the township containing it), nor is it a true marsh. It was created by some efficacious damming to the gratification of numerous coots and mudhens that seek the cover of knee-high shrubs. Resident ducks keep them company while transients drop in through spring and fall, to be met in the latter season, regrettably, by a barrage of shot.

Arrangements with the Ministry of Natural Resources resulted in my getting a coot's-eye view from the bow of a canoe propeled by Supervisor Arnie O'Donnell. Early in our meandering travels, Arnie said what I heard as: "That looks like a plane up there." Half-turning, I found him scrutinizing the heavens through his binoculars, so I shifted my gaze skyward, only to wonder how he held such a responsible position in the provincial ministry. Undoubtedly there was a plane up there, a Cessna, I judged, on some mission unknown to us. But why the song-and-dance about a commonplace occurrence? A little later we landed on a sort of island, already occupied by the first dowitcher to be recorded in the marsh. Having duly placed that event on record, Arnie asked, "Do you think that really was a crane up there?"

Crane! And I missed it! The flying cross was much higher up than the plane I could see so easily. I felt as cheated as I had when I was able to see only a few wing-beats of a small white gull before it passed out of the range of my office window. I have felt ever since that that was as close as I'll ever get to an ivory gull.

The northernmost race of the sandhill crane is a bird of the Canadian and Alaskan tundra that migrates chiefly through the midwest flyway to the coastal marshes of the south. While it occurs regularly along the west side of Hudson Bay and therefore in Ontario on migration, it is of only historical occurrence in the settled part of that province. And so it is high on the desiderata of present-day Ontario birders.

A large version, once specifically distinct, was the original sandhill crane, a resident of the prairie region of Canada and the northern United States, but now extirpated from the northern half or more. The small tundra bird was separated as the little brown crane, while one of intermediate size, called the Florida crane, still abides in the prairie region of Florida and adjacent Georgia. All have been united as a common species, taking their name from the largest form.

In the Okefenokee Swamp of Georgia, our guide worked his way from the old Suwanee Canal into a cul-de-sac, rose cautiously, then apologetically informed us that because of the drought, no cranes were present in an area almost invariably frequented by them. Near-misses of sandhill cranes would seem to be my lot, but I have, fortunately, seen them elsewhere.

The sandhill crane is a conspicuous bird of the Aransas Marshes of Texas, where it is greatly outnumbered by the larger and paradoxically much rarer whooping crane. There, as elsewhere in winter, it is truly a marsh bird. Its summer home is more akin to a bog, while on migration it feeds on open prairies and the unending grain fields of the midwest.

All cranes have an odd mating ritual anthropomorphized as dancing, a grotesque movement of wings and feet that can only have been the inspiration of the war dance of Plains Indians. It is a mannerism similar to certain habits of other birds that must take place to initiate the pairing-mating-nesting sequence. If it is lacking, the sequence does not commence. For that reason, in order to induce a captive sandhill crane to incubate purloined eggs, its keeper had to engage in an arm-flapping, foot-stomping dance with it to get the bird in the proper frame of mind. As I watch dancing on television today, I can visualize getting an entire flock in the pairing mood.

This is the bird that has given its name so mistakenly to our great blue heron, an error first committed by early settlers and continued down through many generations by the uninformed. It was an unpardonable offense because the birds are alike only superficially. The heron is a loner, flies with head pulled back on its shoulders and has only discordant squawks for calls. The cranes move about in flocks (of very large size in early times), trumpet a resonant *gar-oo-oo-oo* and fly with neck outstretched and with a faster, less ponderous wing-beat. In addition, flocks fly in V's or in long lines, showing widely separated feathers at the wing tips. The settlers should surely have known better, especially as they left behind in their homeland the gray heron that differs from ours only by the absence of chestnut in neck and thighs, and the common crane, as gray as ours but with a white stripe on the sides of its black head and neck. It might be added that they made no such confusion in their native lands.

Nest: A large, flat structure of aquatic vegetation built up in a marsh or bog. Eggs: 2, pale brownish, obscurely marked darker brown, sub-elliptical, smooth, slightly glossy. Incubation: 30-32 days, by both sexes. Food: Tubers, grains, worms, insects, frogs, lizards, snakes and small rodents.

Sandhill Crane

G. LOW 83 —

American Avocet

Recurvirostra americana

Breeds on the Great Plains of the U.S. and southern Canada. Winters on the plains of the southern U.S. and the Pacific coast of Mexico.

Among the loveliest bird sights I have ever seen were: A flock of roseate spoonbills on the far side of a Florida pond, their delicately tinted plumage reflecting the rays of a dying sun; the stately progress of long-striding flamingos marching in unison; and the side-sweeping advance of a group of avocets as they worked over pond waters as a farmer mows with a scythe.

Birds exhibit truly diverse feeding habits, some seeming to be fruitless endeavors. We can easily see the success of warblers and vireos who make few mistakes in their insect collecting; and we may note that finches and sparrows use little energy as they forage for seeds. We see the robin miss one now and then and realize the kingfisher must return home with its wings spread far apart as he tells the story of the one that got away. The air-hammer motions of the dowitcher must connect as often as does the groping bill-tip of a snipe. But the avocet, like the black skimmer, must trust to luck more than any other species.

The group I saw that evening was in a ragged line, bill so nicely upcurved that the birds were able to keep the end at or just below the surface of the water while maintaining the body in a horizontal plane. As they moved forward, the bill was swept from side to side, somehow making contact with swimming organisms.

When not feeding, avocets will be found loafing on some sand or mud flat, usually choosing one surrounded by water. At a distance, especially when size is deceptive, a resting flock of avocets may be passed by as a group of idle gulls. It is wise, then, to scrutinize all such flocks of indolent birds as they may not be what you think; or, if you have guessed correctly, they may contain a rarity in their midst. In my experience, a flock of avocets bedded down on an island suggests the incongruity of a snowfall more so than does a flock of gulls or terns, but I don't know why.

Avocets are aberrant shorebirds, exhibiting many traits common to a number of that diverse group of birds. They not only use a scythelike motion of the bill in feeding but also pick and snatch with a dexterity equal to any sandpiper. And, like the sandpiper, they swim and dive well, although not habitually. Also, they have the unusual ability to light on and even take off from the surface of water. While swimming they will tip up as well as any mallard; and if wading, they will discard their usual sedate manner and, with wings partially opened, give chase to a flying or swimming insect. The last action reminds us that like many shorebirds, they have the entrancing habit of holding wings aloft for a moment after alighting.

The world's four species of avocets (to which we can add the two kinds of related stilts) have little originality in their calls, all sticking closely to a yelping note which has led most if not all to be given the cognomen "yelper." Our bird also gives a guttural *whuck-whuck-whuck* in a voice not in keeping with its general appearance.

The American avocet likes ponds and lakes with margins rather devoid of vegetation, which may suggest that it is not primarily a marsh bird But marshes and marshlike conditions are a prerequisite. This bird is found in waters alkaline or slightly saline, and is a common inhabitant of

the ponds within coastal marshes and sometimes even on marine shores, as well as the sloughs of the midwest.

One would expect the American avocet's closest relative to be the pied avocet of the Old World, both species being the only avocets found in the northern hemisphere. To the contrary, our avocet is more nearly related to the geographical-ly distant red-necked avocet of Australia.

Nest: A sparsely lined scrape on the ground by water. Eggs: 3-5 (4), brownish-buff sparsely spotted and blotched black, subelliptical to oval, smooth, non-glossy. Single-brooded. Incubation: 22-24 days, by both sexes. Food: Small marine invertebrates, and mollusks, crustaceans and insects.

Greater Yellowlegs
Tringa melanoleuca

Both species breed in the tundra and muskeg of North America, the range of the lesser straddling that of the greater; both winter from the southern U.S. south to Argentina (lesser) and the tip of South America (greater).

The two yellowlegs (and the two scaups and a few other "twin" species) were, I suspect, placed on earth simply to test our ability to combat frustration. Distressingly alike, tantalizingly dissimilar, they are the bane of the tyro and very often of the expert birdwatcher. The latter thought struck me forcibly when, many years ago, I was tabulating field checking cards at the Royal Ontario Museum in Toronto. From the date, locality and similarity of observations, I realized I had a batch of cards from the seven expert individuals making up a field party; and that three of them had seen a single greater yellowlegs and three had seen a lesser yellowlegs. The odd man out, whose card stated he had seen a solitary sandpiper, ultimately switched, mercifully, to mammalogy.

While the various differences will be found in the better bird books, the best way to distinguish the two birds is to have at least one of each in the field at the same time. When at Oak Hammock, Manitoba, I returned to my car to find my wife and a stranger, a gentleman from Scotland, draped over the engine hood studying an illustration of the two birds while she expounded on their differences. The stranger, experienced in British birds, was an appreciative listener, both to my wife and then to me, when I added a few comments on the birds' more subtle differences. Then, having done my duty so far as I was able, I strolled away, rounded a knoll, took one glance at the marsh in front of me, and returned on the run. "There are a greater and a lesser side by side

Lesser Yellowlegs
Tringa flavipes

around the hill! Hurry!" I extend such courtesies only to gentlemen from Scotland.

The two yellowlegs differ in size, but as the dimensions of a large lesser will approach those of a small greater, identification based on this criterion may be a risky procedure when only one species is present. The bill of the lesser is straight, slim enough to suggest that of a stilt sandpiper or Wilson's phalarope, both of which, in fall dress, can add to the confusion. The longer, stouter bill of the greater *usually* seems upturned at the tip. But, as Palmer states that the bill of an *occasional* lesser is also slightly upturned, we are back very much to square one.

Both birds snatch rather than probe for food, picking up morsels from land or water with a stabbing motion. My impression is that the greater does so the more frequently and is more inclined to get wet right to its belly. And therein may lie the explanation of its slightly upturned bill. For one thing, it will sweep the waters with a scythelike motion, avocet fashion. Moreover, I watched a group in a tidal pool at Bahia Chita, Texas, running about almost madly, the entire bill submerged but held close to horizontal, as they chased topminnows or some other stranded small fish. As a turned-up nose has the advantage over an aquiline one in the parlor game of shoving a peanut over a rug, so is an upturned bill better than a straight one when chasing minnows swimming near the surface of the water. In a millenium or two, the greater yellowlegs may have a bill as deeply upcurved as an avocet's. Check it out later, if you are the questioning sort.

If only an explanation for its so-called bobbing was as readily forthcoming! In effect, it is the tail that bobs, not the head, for, while the rear end is lowered, the neck is lengthened, becoming at the

same time more erect. The action is more frequently observed in nervous birds but cannot be explained away as has the tilting of the spotted sandpiper, which is said to be an imitation of wavelets lapping on a beach.

Being the larger bird, the greater will wade into deeper water, where it may encounter weedy growth. To rid itself of such a nuisance, it has been seen to raise a foot and kick vigorously.

Both yellowlegs are, to some extent, birds of the marsh; not of the impenetrable reed-grown areas tenanted by rails, but of its edges and the shallow, open water away from the margins. Mud flats therein or the borders of lakes and streams are favorite feeding or resting places. The growing number of foul ponds arising from sewage disposal or water purification are well-nigh irresistible. In summer, when nesting, which both do well to the north, the greater likes forested muskeg, the lesser, burnt forest south of the taiga. Although both birds exhibit great alarm when a nesting territory is invaded, nests are rarely found. It is at this time that the birds perch precariously on slender tree branches, calling even more incessantly than when danger, real or otherwise, threatens a migrating flock.

The number of syllables in the calls of birds in flight offers a clue to their identity. While the note of both sounds like *phew*, the greater gives it as a series of three or four notes, the lesser confining its call to just one or two. But sometimes you will meet a greater that can't count to three or a lesser that can go well beyond. When the number of syllables differs from the norm, the sounds will be louder or softer than in the flight call, the various nuances apparently having some meaning to the birds.

Also common to both is a *two-hee*, a rolling yodel that never fails to conjure up memories of

Lesser Yellowlegs

G. LOW 82 - ©

waves of undulating reeds or the wash of rollers on a shimmering strand. Alarm feeding birds, and the conversational murmuring coming from a flock, will change from the single, soft *chup* or *cup* to a hurried, more emphatic series of the same note. A sweetly plaintive song, which given by the greater sounds like *wee-der?* and by the lesser like *pill-a-wee*, is heard only in the north, where — both incessantly snap — *kip* (lesser) or *kek* (greater) when their privacy is invaded. The greater also calls *tee-urk* at such times.

Neither is solitary in habit, but the greater tends to move in flocks of no more than a dozen or so, whereas the lesser might gather one hundred strong. Both associate readily with each other and with other waders, while the lesser may nest in loose colonies.

Nest: A depression on the ground, usually lined with grass or leaves and often near a log, stump or small tree on a wooded ridge. Eggs: 4, buff, spotted and blotched browns (chiefly about the larger end), pyriform to oval, smooth, slightly glossy. There is too little difference in the size of the eggs to help in identification. Incubation: 23 days, by the female alone. Food: Worms, mollusks, crustaceans, insects and larvae, small fishes, and tadpoles.

Willet

Catoptrophorus semipalmatus

Breeds on the Great Plains of central Canada south to the central U.S., on the Gulf coast; and on the Atlantic coast of Nova Scotia and the U.S. Winters on both coasts of the southern U.S. south to Brazil.

The willet may be comparable to a Plain Jane whose rarely given smile is truly dazzling. To provoke her mirth is to transform her into a Miss World contestant. Induce the willet to raise its wings and the bird becomes not necessarily beautiful or even dazzling, but certainly one of our most striking birds.

It seems to me that whenever I visit Atlantic strands the first bird I see will be a willet. Not that it is abundant (neither is it rare), as large birds never are numerous; but because its wings, flashing black and white — whether the bird is in flight, has just landed or is merely showing off — positively scream for attention.

Then, when the wings are closed and this neon sign is turned off, the bird returns to near obscurity, a transformation from a highly visible object to one blending subtly with sand and shadow, marsh and dune. This must surely be the same lifesaving device as the white outer tail-feathers of the junco, which so baffle a pursuer when the bird lands in a bush, closes its tail and seems to disappear from sight.

The first time my wife met the willet was in the New Jersey marshes many years ago. Noticing she was peering about in a puzzled manner, I asked what she was looking for. "The whip-poor-will," she replied. That made two confused people, until I associated her perplexity with the reiterated *pill-will-willet* which came incessantly from several birds that resented our intrusion. In my wife's lexicon, the bird has since been "Willy

Willet." (Strangely, one W. Willet, M.D., lived not far from us at one time.)

The willet endured, and barely, the hard times experienced by almost all shorebirds until regulation forbade some if not all shooting. Willets were under double pressure. Not only did their flesh make a palatable dish, one more substantial than a sparrow-sized least sandpiper, for example, but their eggs were even tastier. And as the birds nested within reach of the well-populated east coast of the United States, the numbers of willets declined to near zero. They have recovered nicely, and now you will hear Dr. Willy Willet wherever a sand beach separates the United States from the Atlantic Ocean. To that we can happily add Canada, where in Nova Scotia the population has greatly increased in the past three decades or so.

Canada, though, always did have a good willet population, as the species has a race in the interior prairie region where, of course, its range extends southward into the central United States. Every time I see or hear a willet in its prairie home I look in vain for the endless vista of cresting rollers, only to see instead waves of grass. It is only these prairie birds, apparently, that winter in North America, either on the California coast where the willet is unknown in summer, or on the Atlantic, which trades its nesting willets for birds from the west.

One doesn't have to be around willets very long before realizing that the species belongs to the tattler group, the same enclave that claims the yellowlegs, redshanks and greenshank. The willets' musical *pill-o-will-willet* will start at the first sound of your footfall and continue until every other kind of bird has either ducked out of sight or gone elsewhere. Old-time gunners and present-day birders have one thing in common: a healthy dislike at times for this telltale of the marshes.

The flight of the willet is said to be ducklike, a characteristic I have never observed, perhaps because of the distraction of its vivid wing-pattern. I was always aware of its strength in the air, with wing-beats rather slow and heavy for a shorebird; and also aware that it sometimes sails on set wings and occasionally hovers like an ungainly falcon. One flight characteristic is that confusion is rampant during landing approach, as if mixed-up air controllers, faulty direction signals and hidden landmarks were creating problems in the cockpit. Especially confused birds have landed in Sweden and France.

A grounded willet is very unlike the yellow-legs, whose posture tends to be less upright. If the willet's blue-gray rather than yellow legs are not discernible, the fact that its forebody is higher than the rear will be noted. And all the while, its bill will be held more nearly horizontal.

Nest: A depression on the ground, lined with grass. Eggs: 4, olive-buff, spotted and blotched shades of brown (chiefly about the larger end), smooth and fairly glossy, pyriform to oval. Incubation: 22-26 days, by the female, although it is assumed that the male takes over at night. Food: Seeds, leaves and roots of grass; worms, mollusks, crustaceans, insects and small fishes.

Willet

G. LOW 82-

Whimbrel

Numenius phaeopus

Breeds in the tundra of the northern hemisphere. Winters from the coasts of the southern U.S. to Brazil and Chile; and from the Mediterranean Sea southward.

In the United Kingdom, where the whimbrel was doubtless a popular target for the falconers of old and may even have been served (scarcely under glass, of course) on the original Round Table, the bird is popularly called "titterel." The fanciful name stems from its rippling whistle, a rapid repetition of the syllable *ti*. Strung together, *tititititi*, as the bird does it, you have a good example of a titter. Every dweller of the high-lands will give unequivocal affirmation to there being seven notes, never more, never less, in the bird's call. But no less an authority than Brian Vesey-Fitzgerald states that while he has heard many a whimbrel, all of which repeated the syllable, he never heard one call seven times! Whether the fault lies with the whimbrel or the listener is not known, but obviously counting is a lost art in one part of the world.

Our bird, long known as the "Hudsonian curlew," is now considered to be the same species as the Old World whimbrel, the chief distinction being that birdwatchers from the British Isles to a long distance eastward are accustomed to seeing whimbrels flash a rump of white. Our bird has a plain brown lower back, a slight variation from the birds of Siberia that have a spotted dark rump. As near as I can ascertain, none of the three subspecies is addict-ed to calling exactly seven times.

During their brief nesting season, the birds frequent the tundra close to both the tree line and marshes. Then, in common with the shore-birds nesting there, the young are left to their own devices and the hordes of insects their obliging parents feel would be in short supply if they remained. These older ones head south, tittering as they go, visiting prairies, uplands, lakeshores and marshes for inland resting and feeding, and tidal flats and salt marshes when near the coasts. Birds of the year follow at a later date.

The migrating flocks are never large, twenty birds possibly a good number these days, although larger assemblages have occurred and still do. They make short work of the many miles they traverse, the slow but strong and steady wing-beats the envy of consumers of expensive gasoline. If you have never seen a whimbrel, you will have little difficulty recognizing one because of the power it exudes in the air, the habit of a flock flying in long straggling lines or in V's that have an irritating tendency to become other letters of the alphabet. And, of course, the long, decurved bill to the fore and the equally long legs stretched out behind are almost deciding factors. The doubt rests in the similarity of the long-billed curlew.

While the latter bird's length of bill and length overall are greater, these two factors are poor criteria. To be certain of identification, one must give close attention to the underwing — cinnamon in the long-bill, buffy in the whimbrel — to separate them with certainty. One Ed Mouncey demonstrated the difficulty. He wrote me of having had a small flock of curlew rest and feed near his summer home in Muskoka, Ontario, two different years (showing something of the faithfulness birds have to productive localities, this area being good blueberry country), and sent what I considered to be almost excellent pictures. I failed to see the characteristic head stripes of whimbrel and so thought the birds long-bills. But Dr. Earl W. Godfrey, the guru at Canada's National Museum, and to whom the slides were submitted, was unable to give a conclusive opinion, partly because none of the birds condescended to hold the wing uplifted, in which

event the shade of the underwing would have been revealed.

This flock, presuming it consisted only of whimbrel, was doubtless part of the population that nests on the west side of Hudson Bay, where visitors to Churchill dodge polar bears to see tundra bird species, including whimbrel. Its migratory path takes it to the St. Lawrence River and thence to the extensive marshes of the Atlantic coast, where the birds look askance at human intruders from August through May. The other population winters along the Pacific shores of California and nests in northwest Alaska and adjacent Canada. Percy A. Taverner, Dr. Godfrey's predecessor, postulated that a third population must have existed between the two at one time, only to be wiped out by some catastrophe.

In the heyday of this Eskimo curlew, the whimbrel was the rarest of the three curlews occurring in eastern North America. Taverner reasoned that the whimbrel benefited from the slaughter of the Eskimo curlew and the decimation of the long-bill. Little distinguishes the three ecologically, so the whimbrel easily took over when the numbers of the other two fell through hunting pressure.

The whimbrel has been further helped because it not only traverses fewer built-up areas on migration, but also because it avoids long ocean routes, because of its wilder, warier nature, and because it forms small flocks. The Eskimo curlew had to contend with the vicissitudes of weather over oceans and pot-hunters ready to shoot anything capable of being cooked.

Nest: A leaf- or lichen-lined depression in grass or moss or on a tussock, in exposed situations. Eggs: 4, olive-buff, spotted and blotched shades of brown (chiefly about the larger end), oval to pyriform, smooth, slightly glossy. Incubation: 26-27 days, by both sexes. Single-brooded. Food: Cloudberries, crowberries, huckleberries and blueberries; worms, mollusks, crustaceans and insects.

detail:
Laughing Gull
page 152

Least Sandpiper

Calidris minutilla

Breeds in the Canadian tundra and on certain islands in the mouth of the St. Lawrence River, and in Newfoundland. Winters from the southern U.S. to Peru and Brazil.

Introduction to the least sandpiper came fairly early in my birding years, my then almost untrained eye picking up a flock of fifty or more that peppered the exposed flats of one of Toronto's watercourses, shriveled by summer's heat and drought. Seeing so many two-legged probing carbon copies at once left little visual impression, but I was impressed in another way. Here it was only July 21, yet these mites were enjoying a stopover on their *fall* migration, a season I was not prepared to entertain for another month or more. Subsequently, I found the gap between the last spring date and the first of fall to be so slight as to sometimes cast doubt on the season of record. Why is the erstwhile companion of Celia Thaxter in such a rush to leave its summer home?

Like the many other species of shorebirds that breed in the Arctic and near Arctic, where the summer is deplorably short, the least sandpiper must cut its love- and home-life to a minimum. To do so, courtship is under way during the latter stages of the spring migration, with the quivering-winged male circling his fancy of the moment. If that particular moment becomes a season, pair-bond is cemented well before the two reach their boggy breeding grounds. To save further time, nest construction is minimal, a few turns of the body in a few wisps of grass carried to a shallow depression. In three weeks' time the young hatch, almost at once nimble of foot, to be abandoned by their parents in a matter of days, a seemingly heartless procedure but one inclined to defeat nature. Abundant as is the insect life in those high latitudes, the supply is still not enough for both young and adults in the latter stages of the year's hatch. So, to ensure ample food for their offspring, parents quickly band together and head southward, knowing their own needs will be taken care of by midsummer's larder "up south," as they say down north. Just how the young follow their parents, navigating a course they have never known, is a puzzle we may never unravel.

The least sandpiper, our smallest shorebird, is a bird of mud flats rather than sand beaches, with a preference for one with a little cover. Inland grassy meadows and grass-edged mud flats of watercourses and ditches are also ports of call on migration. The least's nesting in marshy cover when home has been established south of the mossy, sedgy bogs of the north that attract the bulk of the tribe qualifies it as a marsh bird. You will not, of course, find it sequestered like a rail. It is, rather, in or by that part of a marsh where cover is short enough that the bird can peer over it with just a little stretching.

He is a cheerful little fellow, the chickadee among shorebirds, always found in a small coterie of his order. The almost indistinguishable semipalmated and western sandpipers are his favorite companions, but if need be, he will join sanderlings, small plover, turnstones and phalaropes. Regardless of his associates and how widely scattered his own kind may be while feeding, all the least sandpipers at that particular diner will quickly group when disturbed, to fly off in a compact, wheeling flock that flashes white, then dark, as it banks and swerves as one entity. If reassurance quells anxiety, the flock will return to the bounty it had left. When repose is indicated, least sandpipers remain aloof from the others, bedding down on the higher, stonier

G. LOW 83 —

portions of the beach where their brown forms are lost among the pebbles.

Much as the chickadee is spokesman for his woodland group, so is the least sandpiper along the shores — although he does receive considerable endorsement from the other kinds of small sandpipers which are collated under the name "peep." The commonly heard identification flight call of the least sandpiper, a high-pitched *preep*, comes close to paraphrasing that collective name. It is a squeaky edition of the semipalmated's call, but with greater attention given the *ee* sound. Flushed birds, zigzagging away like little snipe, call *quee-quee-queet*, while a flock wheeling to return to a point of disturbance gives a series of *chu* notes. Few of us are favored to hear the *kreeo-wee* of a bird disturbed at the nest; we must settle for the sweet but tinny twittering of an enraptured male given when hovering on quivering wings, twenty feet above his intended, during a pause on migration in spring.

And only those observers willing to brave the lancets of zillions of mosquitoes will see the least sandpiper at his histrionic best, actually falling over himself as, with pitiable cries, he leads an unwanted beast from nest or young. Like others of the group, he will, at times, invite attention by running through grass, wings outthrust to resemble forelimbs, simulating the race of a tiny rodent.

On migration, though, he is one of our most confiding birds, ever allowing close approach and, it is said, snatching food lying by your foot, provided you refrain from sudden movements. I can appreciate the thrill so experienced as I have twice had semipalmated and western sandpipers so close to my boots that my camera was ineffective. It was also a pleasure, on those memorable occasions, to be so close as to see the webbing between the toes of those two species, a characteristic with which the least is not endowed.

When the presence or absence of this feature cannot be seen (and rest assured, it is seen in the field rarely more than once in a lifetime), we must be guided by other characteristics, such as the tiny, tapering bill, longer and more slender than that of the semipalmated and western sandpipers. The least is darker above than the former, tending to brown rather than gray, and while it might have some ruddiness like the western, it has no droop in the bill. The breast of the least is buffy and more distinctly streaked than either of the others. The legs of the least sandpiper are yellowish or greenish, those of the semipalm, western, and similar but still larger Baird's sandpiper, black; but too often lighting conditions conspire to add color-blindness to our failings. It does help, though, to know that the least, which looks like a small pectoral sandpiper, favors marsh and mud, the semipalm and western, sand. But all of us, and especially the novice, will meet up with exceptions.

Nest: A depression on the ground, in grass, a plant tuft or a mossy hummock; sparsely lined with grass and leaves. Eggs: 4, pale buff, spotted and blotched, sometimes heavily, with browns, pyriform to oval, smooth and glossy. Both parents tend the young, the male doing most of the incubating. Single-brooded. Food: Worms, mollusks, crustaceans and insects.

Pectoral Sandpiper

Calidris melanotos

Breeds in the tundra from Siberia east to Hudson Bay. Winters in South America, Australia and New Zealand.

If the pectoral sandpiper nested, even rarely, in Scotland, it would easily take honors as the Scottish national bird. On the male, concealed by the feathers of the throat and breast, is a fold of skin that, ordinarily, looks like a dewlap if it can be seen at all. In spring, when procreation is the chief interest of the birds, the male will inflate this bag until its size seems doubled. Then, expelling the air much as the piper squeezes the bag of the Scottish musical instrument with his arm, the bird *too-oos* all over the tundra. Like the piper, he hoots on the move, flying about and over prospective mates (the guy's a reprobate); but he also defies Highland tradition by piping standing still. The pectoral, however, is not a Scottish bird, although the species visits the Old World more than any other North American shorebird.

Shorebird? Not an exact definition. It visits the shore only if the beach has growths of grass or if marshlike conditions are just back of the water's edge. In recent years, my wife and I, touring southern Ontario looking for early spring migrants, have stopped because some rough pasture, an unkempt field or land more abandoned than merely lying fallow, has contained large, streaked "sparrows" playing hide-and-seek with us. Then, one would "up-scope," typical sandpiper bill screaming our error, long neck — longer than that of other streaky-brown sandpipers — proclaiming the bird the pectoral.

Invariably, too, we would be surprised by the number of birds present. Only one or two would be seen at first; then a movement would reveal another here, the sweep of binoculars would produce a sprinkling there. A chummy group when moving through the air, but not quite so at the dinner table. Descending to feed, the flock immediately scatters, each bird to himself.

Had we entered the field the birds would have crouched, freezing to avoid our prying eyes. But, step too close to one and it (and no others) would have taken off, a miniature snipe, both in appearance and in zigzagging flight. The call, in fact, a reedy *krrriek*, is reminiscent of a snipe's, but only vaguely so; even in print, it cannot be confused with a snipe's harsh *scaip*.

Toronto's Sunnyside Beach was good pectoral ground in my younger days, but you would never find the birds tripping along the waterline like semipalmated or least sandpipers. (The pectoral is a large edition of the latter.) Instead, pectorals would be back of the shoreline, where long grass and shallow pools dampened the feet of the unwary. A few weeks ago, I found one on a newly formed headland across the bay from the old sandy shore, patrolling a pseudo-beach of mud and grass. The date was June 20, for one of the latest spring dates in my records.

Strangely, while the pectoral is one of the earliest sandpipers to come north in spring it seems reluctant to winter in the northern hemisphere and goes about as far south as it can find land in South America, a very long trip, especially if it has commenced in Siberia, the starting point of some birds.

When sandpipers were invented, they all came out of the same mold, little imperfections in the process creating slight irregularities from the norm, all of which help with identification. Something went awry in the pectoral's case, as witness the aforementioned bagpipes. The second flaw in its makeup is that, while streaked below as so many sandpipers are, at least in some season, the pectoral's streaks end abruptly, just where that dewlap also calls it quits. It is as though a tailor with an uncanny eye for accuracy had run sharp scissors across the streaking for an effect not equaled among sandpipers.

"Krieker," the bird is called, with good reason. "Little snipe" is another good name, as typical snipe habitat is pectoral habitat too. And any name qualified by "grass" is also good. But, be not misled. Pectorals resort to marshes, be they fresh or salt, of typical marsh grass or the black grass to its rear.

Nest: A depression on the ground, often well hidden under a tree or bush; lined with grasses, leaves and sedges. Eggs: 4, buffy, blotched and spotted browns, most heavily about the larger end, pyriform to oval, smooth and slightly glossy. Incubation: 21-23 days, by the female alone, the male sometimes appearing to defend young. Food: Seeds (rarely), worms, mollusks, crustaceans and insects.

Pectoral Sandpiper

G. LOW 82 —

Short-billed Dowitcher

Limnodromus griseus

Breeds in Alaska and Canada from near the tree line south to the northern part of the Canadian Prairie Provinces. Winters in the southern U.S. south to Brazil and Peru.

The greater and lesser scaup, the greater and lesser yellowlegs, the northern and Louisiana waterthrushes and the short-billed and long-billed dowitchers are but a few of the "paired" species which, if you are a devotee of Darwin, you are sure evolved one from the other. The two dowitchers are so similar that it would seem their separation was comparatively recent. In ornithological terms they went their divergent ways not so many years ago, on the edict of the American Ornithologists' Union, when that august body was convinced two species were involved.

Featherwise, there is little to distinguish them, all the so-called field marks being ones of degree. If you are unfamiliar with dowitchers it helps but little to know that one is darker than the other. The long-billed dowitcher does have barred flanks where the short-billed shows streaks; but an observer must be endowed with sharp eyes or be luckily very close to catch such features distinctly. The long-billed species does have a beak averaging longer, but the slight difference is compounded by the disconcerting fact that a long-billed dowitcher with an extremely short bill will have a shorter appendage than a short-bill with a long bill. After such a gem of clarity, best forget it. But, if you can persuade the bird to talk, all doubt will be removed. The short-bill's usual call is a low, mellow whistle of one or more syllables (usually three) sounding like *dowitch* or *dowitcher*, which to some ears sounds like *deutscher*, a bit of bastard German.

The long-bill sticks to a more avian language, giving a piping *keek*, sometimes alone, sometimes in short series.

The dowitchers (there is a third species, even more snipelike, in Asia, by the way) seem to be the connecting link between snipe and sandpipers and are one of the few species of the shorebird suborder to refute the rule of long bill, long legs. Obviously, if a bird has long legs its bill must be oversize in order that the bird may reach the earth and the food found thereon. The dowitchers have the long bill and much of the markings of a snipe, but they move about on short legs disproportionate not only to the bill but also to the body.

Again, while they emulate snipe by feeding in marshy areas, they are not averse to joining other, more typical shorebirds in the shallows of ponds, pools or what-have-you. But where the snipe is a solitary bird, the dowitchers must have company — and of their own kind. The various peeps commonly gather in dozens, even hundreds; the dowitchers form only a good handful, ordinarily five to ten. But they form such a compact flock one suspects family ties are difficult to break. The tight little group is reminiscent of the saying referring to humans: "The family that plays together, stays together." Of dowitchers, change "plays" to "feeds" and you will have succinctly expressed the reason for their togetherness. The flock does not fly with the same degree of unison as a flock of peep; after all, the birds are much larger and their flight path more difficult to control. But at the dinner table the seating is very close.

The dowitcher, as already stated, has some of the markings of a snipe, but it lacks the latter's

G. LOW 81 — ©

heavy crown striping and has a white lower back that runs in a point halfway to the head. In spring the bird is as red below as a robin, a hue missing from the snipe's attire. If none of these far-from-subtle differences makes any impression, the manner of feeding should. The snipe probes the mud deeply, keeping the bill buried for an appreciable length of time as its sensitive bill-tip feels around for a worm. The dowitcher acts like a sewing machine running amok, probing vertically with quick strokes that must connect with some kind of food else the last dowitcher would have succumbed to starvation eons ago. And thus we see the reason for short legs-long bill, as the food it is seeking is not gathered from the surface but from well below it.

The two kinds of dowitchers accept one another readily on their travels and in winter but, at the same time, prefer slightly different environments. The short-bill is more a salt-water bird when not nesting, and of course it leaves a corner of Alaska to the long-billed version in summer.

Nest: A depression on the ground, lined with grass and leaves. Eggs: 4, buffy olive, marked with browns and grays, oval to pyriform, smooth and slightly glossy. Incubation: Not known; possibly by both sexes. Food: Small marine invertebrates and insects.

Common Snipe
Gallinago gallinago

Breeds in both hemispheres from near the tree line south to the northern U.S., and to the latitude of the Mediterranean Sea. Winters from the northern U.S. south to northern South America, and from southern Europe south to the latitude of central South Africa.

This is the bird we graybeards knew as "Wilson's snipe." Its rechristening came about in 1957, when it was decided it was not specifically distinct from the Old World form after all. But whether the AOU nomenclature committee decided on "common" because the bird is common to both Old and New Worlds, or whether it adopted the name used in England, where it is the most common of the three kinds of snipe there, has not, so far as I am aware, been divulged.

To say the Old and New World birds are subspecies is to imply that they are genetically compatible; but I wonder. Our bird has a tail of sixteen feathers and, while a few of theirs have sported as little as twelve, a few as many as eighteen, the usual number of the Old World form is fourteen. I would imagine that a hen of one subspecies would recoil from a strutting male of the other if his spread tail seemed, to her, to be a deformity.

Usually, we meet the snipe in one of two ways. One is when walking about a marsh or over any kind of wet, open ground where little declivities or grassy or sedgy tussocks make walking difficult. Our concentration in search of good footing is rudely jolted by the explosive rise and equally explosive snort of a brown bird that makes off in such an erratic course it would seem to have selected a damaged corkscrew as a flight plan. We may be fortunate to catch sight of a long bill, which is carried pointing downward, and a short,

somewhat orange tail. The harsh, rasping cry is usually referred to as *scaip* or *es-scape*, both spelled in a variety of ways; but in my estimation, the bird does not enunciate so clearly, nor does it seem to make use of a vowel. I hear it as *tzrrk*.

The other way we may meet a snipe is to not meet it at all! Which certainly requires elucidation. Approaching sundown or during a cloudy day in spring, when near a marsh or bog favored by nesting snipe (and once such a site is used it is given top rating by snipe realtors ever after), we may hear a most peculiar, eerie sound that seems to come from the sky, although its origin is difficult to locate. Nor can we find its author. The mystifying notes, which are wretchedly described by the syllables *whuwhuwhuwhu*, come from a male snipe intent on claiming the territory over which it is flying. The hollow sound has been called a booming, whinnying, humming, bleating, drumming and winnowing, the last describing it best, as it is something like the whistle of a duck's wings in flight. While I have yet to see and hear the Old World snipe, the impression given me by English authors is that, over there, they really do hear a drumming or bleating (Linnaeus named the bird "little goat"), which descriptions were faithfully and incorrectly transposed to the New World bird by American writers.

The sound is produced by a territorially minded male (although females will respond in like fashion) in this way. Rising some 300 feet, he turns sideways and swoops down at a forty-five-degree angle, keeping his tail spread, while the two outer tail-feathers are stuck out to the sides. These feathers, so the theory goes, are vibrated by the strong current of air directed to them by the partly closed wings, which also vibrate. We hear the noise of rushing air as we

G. LOW 83 -

also hear it during the dive of a nighthawk; but in the case of the snipe, the vibrating wings pulsate the airflow just as a flautist plays a trill or as a violinist, whose finger trembles somewhat on the string, changes an otherwise flat note to a vibrant, living one.

A Swedish naturalist by name of Meves reproduced the sound in 1856 by swishing a stick to which he had fastened two snipe feathers. In 1907, Sir Philip Mason-Bahr whirled a feather-bearing cork with the same result. And, about 1920, Eric Parker fastened feathers to an arrow, delightedly hearing the same sound as it fell. But Brian Vesey-Fitzgerald claims that all three English snipe drum, and that only one, the common, has stiff outer tail-feathers. Furthermore, he states they drum not only in the air but also on the ground. Ruminating after a rueful return to the beginning of this treatise, I still insist our erstwhile Wilson's snipe winnows; theirs drums or bleats.

Whatever and however, this love cruise is carried out only over the nesting territory and sometimes at such height we cannot find the author, especially if the light is poor, which it usually is. And that is why you will still not meet the bird.

But the snipe's true love song is a rapid, rail-like, mechanical ticking, sounding like *whit-whit-whit*, or *whit-a-whit-a-whit-a*, in a lengthy series and which, while often given before winnowing, is usually delivered from almost any kind of elevated perch. I drove under such a yacking bird as it swayed on a long, drooping utility wire crossing a highway on the Gaspé Peninsula.

A night-flying migrant, largely crepuscular and very trustful of its mottled plumage to avoid detection by day, a snipe would seem to be found only with the aid of a pointing dog. Fortunately, the bird relents in fall, when it will visit mud flats and shallows to probe the ooze for hidden delicacies it finds with its tactile, slightly movable bill-tip. On a mud flat I know well there may be some eight or ten snipe emulating slow-motored sewing machines. Nor are they above a little ducking, as the head will be submerged up to but not over the eyes, a precautionary measure taken to thwart airborne enemies.

You will not see snipe come; nor will you see them go. You will only be aware that some ground is full of snipe today, completely snipeless the next, as even short flights are made under cover of darkness. Occasionally, one enjoys a more intimate meeting, usually in the vicinity of a nest or young, when the birds will use a distraction display complete with fractured wing-bone. The story that a snipe will carry a young bird between its thighs has some credibility, as I once saw the closely related woodcock moving its young in that manner when my steps were taking me, unknowingly, to their resting place.

Each member of a pair of snipe has a "His" and a "Hers" station within the nesting territory. The male will stick pretty close to "His," the female visiting "Hers" during each incubation break. When the young hatch, the brood is split, although not necessarily evenly, the male taking its quota to "His" stand, the remainder being led to "Hers" by the mother. This is one of the pleasant domestic angles we run into in bird study.

Nest: A depression on the ground, in a tussock of grass or a sedge or mound of moss; lined with grass and leaves. Eggs: 4, olive or olive-brown, heavily blotched and spotted darker browns, oval to pyriform, smooth and slightly glossy. Single-brooded but sometimes double-brooded, especially in the Old World form. Incubation: 19-20 days, probably by both sexes. Food: Algae, aquatic plants, mollusks, earthworms, crustaceans, insects and larvae.

Common Snipe

Wilson's Phalarope
Phalaropus tricolor

Breeds from central British Columbia, the central Prairie Provinces and southern Ontario south to the central U.S. west of Lake Michigan. Winters in South America.

A slough in the west is to the prairie as an oasis is to the arid, sandy desert. For the most part, the surrounding country will be a flat expanse of brown, green or gold, depending on the season and the grain of the moment. The waters of the slough will be dotted with somberly hued ducks and grebes, flashes of color evident only on those occasions a drake condescends to visit the nursery or when the flashy adornments of a grebe reflect the rays of the sun.

Then, careening over the open waters, skimming over the rush- and tule-grown margins, comes a trio of long-legged, long-billed birds. The flight is swift and twisting, the leading bird straining for the utmost in evasive tactics. The two pursuing birds are gaudy of plumage, broadly striped in black and white, chestnut and browns. The pursued presents much the same pattern but its feathers seem worn or faded, as if with age. One would expect the madcap ramble to be accompanied by a cacophony of screams; but, except for the swish of rapidly moving pinions, there is only a hollow *wah-wah-wah* from the pursuers.

On my early summer visits to the Canadian prairies, almost every slough presented much the same spectacle: the courtship flight of Wilson's phalaropes. You'll see the same thing enacted by red-winged blackbirds, robins and orioles. In these three species, it is the chase of a male lusting for a female. But in the case of phalaropes, it is the female that takes the initiative.

Indeed, we would expect the female phalarope to be a heavily structured, deep-voiced individual sporting an incipient mustache, so "masculine" is she in courtship. In one respect, and looking at it from a bird's point of view, we would not be far astray. For the female of not only Wilson's but also of the other two phalaropes is the brightly colored one, the one displaying those physical aspects which, in birds, are usually the exclusive property of the male.

This reversal of colors and actions has been stressed times without number, with the inference that it occurs only in the phalaropes. But it is now known that several species of shorebirds, of which the phalarope is one, are programmed to have the male sex take over most if not all housekeeping detail. Some species, far removed from shorebirds, exhibit the same trait. Les Snyder, my mentor of years ago, found male white-throated sparrows doing most of the incubating if their mate's plumage was the more brilliant.

All three phalaropes have carried the reversal of roles to the extreme, for while the hen initiates the search for a nest site, and while both she and her mate will scratch about such locations, it is the male that prepares the nest proper, which is nothing more than a slight hollow devoid or denuded of vegetation. Once the clutch is complete, the female takes off, to spend her time at the phalarope equivalent of afternoon teas, bridges, matinees and fashion shows. She may even cast morals aside, if she ever had any, and some don't, and enter into another liaison.

Except for a few favored localities in southern Ontario, this phalarope is a bird of the interior,

its visits to salt water being confined to fall and winter and made more commonly on the west coast than the east. Away from the nesting season it has a marked resemblance to the lesser yellowlegs but has legs of greenish-yellow, not bright yellow, along with an unstreaked breast and the so-called phalarope mark back of the eye. Somewhat more active than the yellowlegs, it swims when the other rarely does. On water it performs the phalarope trick of spinning, thus stirring up small organisms.

It is not a very demonstrative bird vocally. In addition to the *wah-wah* given by females intent on even the flimsiest of matrimonial alliances, the most common call is nothing more than a grunt.

Nest: An unlined depression on the ground. Eggs: 3-4 (4), creamy buff-blotched shades of brown, pyriform to oval, smooth and slightly glossy. Incubation: 20-21 days, by the male alone. Food: Aquatic insects.

Laughing Gull

Larus atricilla

Breeds on the Atlantic coast from Nova Scotia south to northern South America, in the West Indies, and on the Salton Sea and Pacific coast of California. Winters on the coasts of the southern U.S. to northern South America.

The use of the term "sea-gull" annoys me considerably. As I have pointed out in more than one newspaper column, the gulls of the world are quite diverse in their choice of breeding habitat, some sticking close to a marine environment, some inhabiting inland lakes and marshes, while one, the gray gull, nests in desertlike regions in South America. But all, at some time of their lives, visit the ocean, so that none has a stranglehold on the term "sea-gull." Still, if any one North American gull deserves the appellation, it is this species. I have twice seen it over Lake Ontario at Toronto and once at Montmorency, Quebec, at which time it was within reach of intrusive salt water in the St. Lawrence River. Otherwise, I have never seen one more than four miles from the ocean.

While preeminently an ocean bird, it stays well within the continental shelf, an habitué of sandy beaches, sand bars, islets and river mouths, and particularly the salt-water marshes, one of its favorite nesting habitats. Yet, while exceptionally numerous about the extensive marshes of New Jersey, it proved singularly rare about equally large marshes I visited in southern Georgia. Nor does it seem common and widespread in the Caribbean, my one record of the species while visiting St. Lucia being a tandem flying about a mile out from that luscious tropical gem. The only inland body of salt water it regularly frequents is the Salton Sea of California. But like many ducks that winter on salt water, it will go inland to bathe in waters free of a saline taint.

When the species is present in numbers you will be constantly aware of it during the daytime. If bird song annoys you in the early hours of the morning, ocean living will not be your cup of tea, although a more appropriate metaphor in Florida, where it is very numerous about the beaches, is "your glass of orange juice." Each daybreak, as birds launch into the air to begin their incessant search for food, they start their strident, staccato *ka-ha-ka-ha*, stopping only when they find a bite to eat and, mercifully, at sundown.

Acute hunger will drive it to garbage dumps but, except for offal thrown from fishing boats (and the entrails may be considered fresh meat rather than carrion), the laughing gull has not the scavenging habits of the herring, ring-billed and large marine gulls of the north. I do not recall having seen a laughing gull pecking at some moribund fish on a beach. Freshly caught fish are preferred, with king crabs topping the menu. It dotes on larger insects such as dragonflies and flying termites, hawking for them like an overgrown swallow; and it will forsake the briny for a field being ravaged by a plow and the grubs it brings to light. Such fields, of course, cannot be too far inland. And coastwise communities sometimes will have a coterie of the birds searching the lawns for earthworms surfacing after a rain.

It is said to follow porpoises herding small fish for their own purposes, and also to rob brown pelicans of their catch. I have been a fascinated spectator at many a pelican plunge but have yet to see a laughing gull take advantage of the pelican's skill. The gull is said to remove a fish from the pelican's pouch as deftly as a slick-handed pickpocket, all the while standing on the head of its unwitting benefactor.

G. LOW 80~ ©

Laughing Gull

It is a very gregarious species, nesting in sometimes large colonies and loafing in small groups on a sand bar, often with many of the several kinds of terns that are found oceanside. Its gregariousness and therefore the ease of capture of large numbers at one time may have led to its near extinction toward the end of the last century. Its feathers were highly desired by the millinery trade, but like other species, chiefly herons, slaughtered for the same reason, it bounded back when such adornments were literally forced out of fashion. But now a new threat to its existence has developed in the upper limits of its breeding range. There the fantastic increase in the herring gull population has forced the laughing gull from favored nesting localities. The laughing one can be easily intimidated by the larger bird as it is not particularly aggressive. In fact, it is rarely given to egg stealing because of its milder nature.

Bonaparte's, Franklin's and the laughing gulls are the common black-headed species of North America. All have a flight lighter and airier than the white-headed gulls such as the herring and ring-billed. But the laughing gull, perhaps our most common black-head, flies in a slightly heavier manner than the Bonaparte's and Franklin's. It is, after all, slightly larger than either. On the water, it floats as high and as lightly as any.

The black of its head is said to extend farther down the nape than in Bonie's or Franklin's, but I have noticed no appreciable difference. Its all-dark upper wing surface is a sure mark, while the laughing is the only mirthful one, if one can describe its call as an expression of jollity. What may be imagined as its song is an elaboration of its incessant cry, a long series of *ka's*, *ha's* and *aah's* intermixed with a few *oh's*. You will have met people like that who respond so well to a story, even a pointless one.

Nest: Sometimes in colonies; in the south, a depression in sand-lined grass or seaweed; in the north, a well-made, substantial cup or platform of grass and seaweed in thick grass or shrubbery. Eggs: 3-4 (3), buff, spotted and blotched brown, subelliptical to oval, smooth and glossy. Single-brooded. Incubation: 20-21 days, by both sexes, but they rely on the sun a great deal. Food: Marine worms, mollusks, earthworms, crustaceans, insects, fishes, and some garbage, offal and carrion.

Franklin's Gull

Larus pipixcan

Breeds in the Great Plains of southern Canada and the northern U.S. Winters on the coasts of Texas and Louisiana and on the Pacific coast from Central America to Chile.

Franklin's gull deserves to be eulogized as much as the California gull, the one that saved early Mormons from starvation and economic ruin by descending on hordes of grain-destroying locusts. But the feat of that western gull was a one-time exploit. The good deeds of Franklin's gull go on year after year, ever since the first plow turned a furrow on the western plains.

The city desk of the daily press, invariably confused on matters of natural history, would label this bird a "sea-gull," just as it does all gull species. But Franklin's spends less time on salt water than most, living its summers far from the host of gulls patrolling the seashore. In fact, some individuals may not spend much time about a sizable fresh-water lake. The bird is, quite positively, a marsh bird, nesting within reed-grown wetlands in hundreds and, more often, thousands.

Marshes, though, are but the bird's bed-chamber or, to be more precise, its nursery. Even while preoccupied with incubating and raising downy young, Franklin's gulls roam the western plains and prairies as much as thirty miles from their chosen homestead, which site may drop out of favor one year, another gaining popularity. On their foraging travels they may drop into a lake here, a slough there, a likely field in this quarter, a promising stream in that, seeking not garbage, the delight of most of the world's gulls, but insects, more and more insects, and their larvae. Some frogs and small fishes restore jaded appetites, while the opportunists to be found in any respectable community may snatch an egg from

under the less-than-watchful care of some other species. But Franklin's has a diet close to wholly insectivorous, except during those few months of winter sojourn along seacoasts.

The farmers in the vast croplands of central North America know well the value of the bird. The birds time their arrival in spring to the opening of the plowing season, but actually, they always did arrive with the break-up of winter. Nevertheless, the coincidence of spring plowing and their reappearance is a happy one, not only from the bird's standpoint but also in the view of the agriculturist. Perhaps the larger and more modern farm equipment, with its gang plows having opened up larger and more dining areas, is responsible for the increase in the species' population. There is no denying that the ground behind a plow will seem blanketed with snow, so numerous are the birds seeking the various worms, grubs and insect larvae exposed by the plowshares. Any right-thinking farmer will realize the birds could be his economic salvation.

After nesting, flocks again visit the fields, this time often accompanied by Bonaparte's gulls; and, settling down within the now standing grain, they will wage war on grasshoppers and locusts, a battle that continues later behind the enormous harvesting equipment as the fields are reduced to stubble. If we could only defeat drought, the western grain growers would have few problems.

But regardless of the season and the size of the flocks on one particular field, small groups of Franklin's gulls seem always in sight, winging over the flat plains, their origin and destination twin mysteries. While driving over the prairies I have invariably found myself with one eye on the road, the other on a flock of birds, until, by craning my neck at a dangerous angle, I would

again determine it was the Franklin's gull that almost sent me into the ditch. With the identity of that bunch established, I would immediately sight another distant one, and another game of road roulette would begin. Then, reaching my destination for that evening and provided I was still in prairie country, I would suddenly realize that the gulls over my inn or the western metropolis playing host for that night were neither herring nor ring-billed gulls, so familiar to me in the east, but more of the west's "prairie pigeon," truly an apt name.

It is at such times that I have been impressed by their apparent silence. Herrings, ring-bills, California, common, and most especially, laughing gulls seem forever screeching. Franklin's is by no means silent, but perhaps it seems so by contrast. Its most characteristic note is a brief succession of *week-as* followed by a similar number of *po-lees*, all with the shrill quality of gulls in general. A louder, almost plaintive call is a nasal *pwaay*. Sometimes one will give a series of shrill *kuks* often softened to a *krrruk*, but on the whole Franklin's gull makes a far better neighbor than a sawmill or shipyard.

This gull is so wedded to the central plains region of North America that not even during the annual spring and fall trek do any more than a handful venture to the Atlantic or Pacific coasts. Some drop off at the Gulf of Mexico and the Gulf of California, but the majority carry on to become the only gull to cross the equator regularly, winding up on the Pacific coast from Ecuador to the southern tip of Argentina. In recent years an increasing number, although still a handful, have been visiting the Great Lakes in late summer, while a couple of birds have made it to Great Britain.

Perhaps their extended migration is possible because they may feed on the wing, as do swallows, swift and other aerial feeders. Certainly their capture of airborne insects is accomplished in a swallowlike fashion, far from the clumsy effort of the ring-billed gull. In the east I have often watched ring-bills attacking a swarm of high-flying gnats, their ponderous acrobatics the antithesis of the practiced ease of the nighthawks attracted to the same bounty.

One of the traits of Franklin's that I find pleasing, even if it may just be the result of forgetfulness, is its concern for its young. With nests more or less floating, young birds must swim immediately on leaving the cradle. If the decision to quit their natal abode coincides with a breeze, the little puffballs are blown about like thistledown. Those that are blown across the lake to the birds nesting on the other side are taken in with wide-open wings, fed and cared for as though always part of the family. If the far shore is too distant for such hospitality to be practiced, the adults on the side of origin will unite to shepherd, urge or cajole the drifters homeward. Recalcitrants are picked up and carried shoreward. Corporal punishment may be administered to obstinate young, but all arrive home safe, albeit a bit bloodied.

Nest: A mass of marsh vegetation floating or nearly so on water up to six feet deep and usually anchored to live marsh growth. Eggs: 3, buff or greenish-brown, spotted, blotched and scrawled dark browns, some in a wreath about the larger end, subelliptical, smooth and slightly glossy. Incubation: 18-20 days, by both sexes. Food: Insects and larvae, small fishes and frogs.

Franklin's Gull

Forster's Tern

Sterna forsteri

Breeds on the Great Plains from central Canada to the northern U.S. Winters on the Pacific coast from central California to Central America; on the Gulf coast; and on the Atlantic coast from Virginia to Florida.

Forster's tern was and still seems to be the forgotten tern of North America. It was known as far back as 1821, when Audubon shot one of thousands wintering at New Orleans. Although he painted it, he apparently did not retain the skin and so was unable to circumvent officialdom to allow his name of "black-billed tern" (*Sterna ludovicianus*) to stand. Later he changed the vernacular to "Havell's tern," after Robert Havell, Jr., who prepared most of his engravings. Since the first name was never accepted, his alternative followed it into oblivion.

Audubon's bird, taken in January, was in winter plumage, the only one known until the travels of William Swainson and John Richardson who, although describing a specimen satisfactorily, thought it was the common tern. In 1834, Thomas Nuttall, noting the differences — easily recognized when the bird is carefully described from a specimen in the hand — based his description on the one contained in Swainson and Richardson's 1831 publication. Nuttall named it after Johann Reinhold Forster, who accompanied Captain James Cook on his second voyage to the Pacific. Not until 1858 was the scientific world given a more satisfactory description, by George N. Lawrence, while the bird's plumage sequences were not known until 1877, when Elliott Coues reviewed the species' life history.

Even yet, it is an overlooked bird, easily passed over by observers who might accord a milling flock of terns but a casual glance, considering them all the common variety. True, it is very like the common tern and, it might be added, also very similar to the roseate and Arctic terns. But while some differences are the subtle ones of degree, others are quite distinctive. First, Forster's is, in summer at least, essentially a marsh bird, whereas the common is given to patrolling the bays and shorelines of oceans and fresh-water lakes and rivers. Forster's slightly larger size, shorter wings and longer, more streaming tail do, of course, aid little in field identification unless both species are together; but its shading is a different matter. The white underparts are without gray anywhere. The tail is gray, almost like the back, with its inner edge darker, whereas that of the common is dark on the outer edge. But the best mark is the flash of silvery white on the inner primaries, a patch not revealed in the flight feathers of the other bird — all an unmarked shade of gray, darkening toward the tips. Eyes tuned for color distinction may note that the bill and feet of Forster's verge to orange, those of the common to red. In young birds and winter adults, Forster's is the only tern to wear a dark patch through the eye, the bar stopping much short of the nape. Young birds are further distinguished by the absence of a bar in the wing. When the two species are in the air together, as they sometimes are, the faster wing-beat of Forster's may be apparent. There is a snap to the shallower stroke, whereas the slower action of the common adds to the illusion of buoyancy, when the bird seems suspended on a string in the hands of a puppeteer.

Unlike the common tern, which is found in most parts of the northern hemisphere, Forster's greater selectivity of habitat restricts it to that part of North America where prairie sloughs abound, although it is also found on the Atlantic

G. LOW 83—

coast of the southern states. While it reaches its wintering grounds of the tropical and near tropical coasts of the eastern hemisphere by traversing a large part of North America, it is not a world traveler, as are many of its relatives. A bird taken in Iceland seems to have been the only one with wanderlust.

A single such wayfarer is in keeping with the species' near-phobia of crowds, for where others nest, rest and winter in large colonies of sometimes thousands, Forster's terns believe in small, scattered groups. Even when nesting, crowding is discouraged, as several yards will be found between neighboring nests. When Forster's is found nesting amid common terns, my guess is that the larger species was there first, the other taking advantage of unclaimed real estate.

Notwithstanding the snap given in the wing-beat, Forster's is still a graceful bird in the air, breaking its quest for aquatic tidbits with a sudden twist as it aligns itself for a dive waterward. This may be such a deep plunge that the bird will disappear completely, shaking itself like a dog on emerging. And often the dive will be a graceful, curving dip, with not a feather dampened. When I was watching a half-dozen or so flying up and down the Frenchman River in southwestern Saskatchewan, near the United States border, I thought the river must have been fished out, as not once did I see a tern dive. Then I realized the birds were hawking for insects, a manner of feeding they employ consistently.

Their grace and beauty are marred by a somewhat repulsive habit which recurs early each spring when, with live food still in short supply, the birds will pick up the long-dead bodies of fish and frogs killed by the movement and ravages of winter's ice.

The appearance, flight and calls of all terns have such a family resemblance that it is safe to assume they broke off from a common ancestor not so many millions of years ago. The call analogous to the common tern's *kee-ar* is spelled by some authors in the same way. But it is lower pitched, harsher and more nasal, so that a rendering including a "z" sound is more acceptable. To me it sounds like *tzeap* or *tzreep*, and is, as many affirm, remarkably like the call of the nighthawk, another aerial insect-catcher. It also has a rapid, peeping *kip-kip-kip-kip*, sounding, as one writer expresses it, like a person clucking to a horse.

Nest: Variable, from a hollow in sand, mud or flattened vegetation slightly lined if at all, to a well-built, substantial cup of grass and reeds lined with finer materials; on the ground, on flattened reeds or on an old muskrat's house that may have as many as five nests. Eggs: 3-4 (3), buff, irregularly spotted, sometimes blotched or scrawled with dark brown and lilac, subelliptical to oval, smooth, non-glossy. Incubation: 23-24 days, by both sexes. Single-brooded. Food: Insects, fishes (dead or alive) and frogs (dead or alive).

Black Tern

Chlidonias niger

Breeds from southern Canada to the central U.S., and in Europe and central Russia. Winters in Central and South America and in Africa.

There is no doubt that the subject of this sketch, the opposite of the fairy tern of the Australasian region, is the black sheep of the family, most of which are white with a gray or silver mantle and a long, rakish cap of black. The black tern's transgressions are, apparently, of such magnitude that the only white remaining is found on the lower belly.

Why was it ostracized? Not because it is a villain. It is no nest robber like its distant relative, the herring gull. Its whole demeanor is as exemplary as that of a mourning dove, although in one respect the two species differ widely. Where the dove can frazzle our nerves with its monotonous, continuous cooing, the black tern is relatively silent; that is, unless you invade its nesting grounds. Then all hades escapes. But this cannot be the reason for its fall from grace, as all terns raise pandemonium when you set foot in the nursery, sometimes becoming so resentful as to draw blood from the unprotected head. At such times their screeching is reminiscent of a chain accident on a highway, when dozens of wheels scream in protest of sudden brake application.

Perhaps the reason for the black tern's downfall is its unfaithfulness. Terns, as a class, are very much attached to the sandy stretch, shingle, island or grassy point they call home during the nesting season, returning year after year until some catastrophe forces them to abandon it. The black tern favors a marsh but, whatever its selection, has so little regard for it, it may not use a particular locality again for several years.

That, however, may be true only in the northern part of its range, from which it migrates very early, rarely remaining into August. Naturally, too, birds nesting near the northern limit will do so in small numbers, raising the possibility that the entire colony can be wiped out on its migratory travels.

The flight of the black tern is near the acme in buoyancy and grace. I say "near" as, to me, the flight of the common tern is lighter. Both species, though, seem to be floating on air like large butterflies, or a paper folded by a schoolboy intent on distracting his class with an imitation of an airplane. One marked difference in the flight is that the common tern plunges into the water for its food; the black is more inclined to pluck its meals from the surface, which suggests, facetiously, that its infrequent bathing brought about its sordid condition.

There is also a marked difference in diet. The common is preeminently a fish eater, the black only occasionally, preferring insects to flesh. Partial to organisms it gathers from the surface, the black dives but rarely. And, totally unlike the common, it is a follower of the plow, picking up grubs and grasshoppers from furrows as deftly as it removes insects from the waves.

I cannot recall seeing a common tern flying over land, except, of course, the area where it nests or rests. But not long ago I watched a black tern feeding over a large, marshy lake, its erratic, nighthawk-like flight interrupted by occasional dives to the surface. Then, its bill presumably full, it turned and headed across not only solid ground, but ground well grown with planted conifers. It was apparently taking the shortest route to a nestful of young.

Its sharp, nasal voice is ternlike but seems to

lack the unearthly screeching of the common and most other terns. Given in flight, it can be monotonous at times, a repetition of the syllable *kik*, becoming a shriller, longer *kreek* if excited or when its nest is approached. An occasional variant is a *klee-ar*, analogous to the common's similar call.

This bird was wiped out as a breeding species of Great Britain when its peoples became too obsessed with the draining of marshes. It serves as one more example of the necessity of maintaining wetlands.

Nest: Constructed of marsh vegetation, floating and anchored to reeds or placed on a muskrat house. Eggs: 2-3 (3), olive-brown, heavily blotched dark browns, oval to subpyriform, smooth and slightly glossy. Single-brooded. Incubation: 19-20 days, by both sexes. Food: Insects, small marine invertebrates and fishes.

Black Tern

detail:
Short-eared Owl
page 166

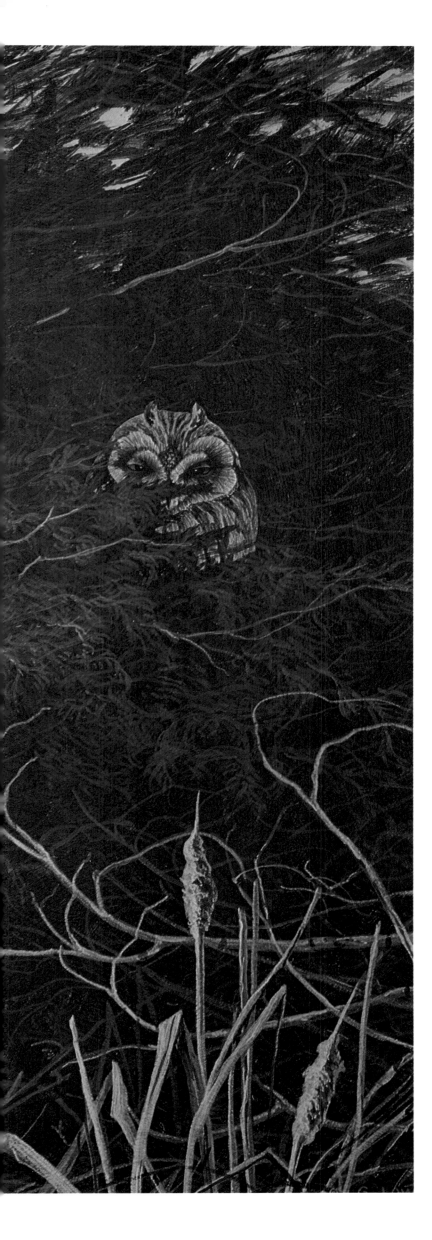

Short-eared Owl
Asio flammeus

Breeds throughout virtually all the world except Africa and India, which it visits in winter. Moves southward in cold weather.

The short-eared owl is, without question, a marsh bird, but only when it lives near a seacoast where extensive salt marshes persist, or in inland areas where large, low wetlands are grown with rushes and similar marsh cover. In winter, if such a marsh is not handy, it will settle for flat lands with a good, grassy overlay. In such places the growth need not be what we consider grass but what we lump together as cereals. The short-eared owl has two further stipulations. Such fields should have the growth reduced to near the height of stubble; and they must contain an abundance of meadow voles, the short-tailed mouselike creature that is the principal sustenance of innumerable kinds of birds, mammals and snakes.

It was the combination of a grassy field and a large quantity of meadow voles that led me to conclude that the short-eared owl is not necessarily a loner, as are all other owls, the long-ear mildly excepted. There were seventeen owls in the concentration I discovered one winter. Later I counted other congregations from three up to fifteen, all with the same community of interest — a taste for meadow voles. Other owls show animosity not only to other species of owls but also to their own kind. Even an owl paired for breeding purposes must be watchful of its mate. The tolerance so evident in the short-ear is shown to a lesser degree by the long-eared owl, indicative of the close relationship of the two. But as the long-ear is both a woods and a night owl, gatherings of that species are not so noticeable. Indeed, any concentration of long-ears will be found to be part of a gathering of its relative.

The short-ear can be quite diurnal, however, although it is likely that the large numbers seen during daylight hours were bred in the far north that knows little darkness during the summer. The birds in the flocks I have met seemed quite at ease in the sun, perching on the flat tops of wooded fence posts or flying about aimlessly, like giant moths.

The buoyant, mothlike flight is so ludicrous in a bird of such bulk that an observer is pardoned for being somewhat stupefied. Once seen, though, it cannot be forgotten. I recognized short-ears a good mile away as they crossed and recrossed a road over which my wife and I were traveling. Even at that distance there was a silence to their flight. Nor does the buoyancy suggest the airiness of a tern. The bulk of the body, the neckless appearance, the broad, rounded wings, all call for a heavy, flapping progress, something you never see in this or any other owl, for that matter. Moreover, the bird seems to be flying with the wing-tips on one plane while the body flaps up and down!

Short-eared owls have converged on vole harvests in more places than near my home. One in particular comes to mind. In Scotland, where the owls had never been seen, they gathered in one area in the hundreds!

While I am amazed at the airy flight of such a bulky bird, I am similarly astounded at the ability of the species to communicate. Assuming a hunting owl finds a bonanza of voles, how does it transmit information to others which may be miles and miles away? They do not move about in flocks. It is only when a bountiful supply of food appears that congregating becomes a fact. Nor do they soar high like vultures who, by their actions on sighting an edible carcass, alert other, distant birds. The short-ear will, indubitably, find its prey at night. Next day the area will be swarming with them.

Except for the fact that the "ears" of short-and long-eared owls are not ears, any more than the "horns" of a great horned owl are protruding bones (they are merely tufts of feathers with no auricular connection), the name, "short-ear," sets it apart from the long-ear very well. Where the tufts are very evident in the long-ear, those of the short-ear are so buried in the crown as to be little more than bumps, a unique adornment. The prominent tufts of the long-ear give it such a feline appearance it is called "cat owl." But the short-ear is not without a catlike visage, short tufts notwithstanding. I became even more aware of that when my son Peter found three roosting in a rather skimpy conifer. Their disregard for nearby traffic and humans equaled their strong resemblance to kittens. The name marsh owl is, however, more appropriate than either short-eared or kitten owl.

Although all owls are generally associated with hooting, this vocal effort is restricted to very few, and the short-ear is not one of them. Instead, it gives a somewhat explosive triplet sounding like *itch-itch-itch*, but which others hear as *wak-wak-wak*. In any event, vocalization is rarely heard away from the nest.

Nest: A depression on a little eminence on the ground, lined with a few weeds and feathers. Eggs: 4-14 (5-7), creamy white, ovate, smooth, non-glossy. Single-brooded. Incubation: About 25 days. Food: Insects, birds and small mammals.

Marsh Wren

Cistothorus palustris

Breeds from central Canada south through the whole of the U.S. Winters in the southern half of the U.S.

As a subject for an essay, the marsh wren is a very poor one. The house wren is very much better, for the incontestable reason that you can see that bird. But see a marsh wren? Oh, sure, if you train a telescope on the top of a distant bulrush or cattail and watch patiently for days.

For the marsh wren is as secretive as any rail, living its life away buried in some marsh where the water is perhaps too shallow for canoeing, the bottom too mucky for wading and the marsh growth so interwoven as to make the whole a fortress more formidable than one surrounded by a moat filled with crocodiles. I doubt if my experience is much different from that of other observers: An occasional glimpse of a bird as it clutches two tall, swaying reeds, tail so cocked as almost to touch its black cap, vituperative clacking from a pulsating throat as it berates my intrusion. Then it is gone.

The alarm sounds like *twu-twu-twu-tsuck*, while the grating scolding note is a single *tsuck*, which continues from one point after another as the bird moves about, its speed showing it is not "tsuck" after all.

When I visited Hopkins' Point, Quebec, the marsh there, for all its grandness, yielded only one marsh wren, visually; but from every corner came the guttural, bubbling, rattling song, testifying to the bird's abundance, especially in habitat of its liking.

The song has been received with mixed feelings, as one author states it is harsh, another that it is musical. Some think the bird is more gifted musically than the house wren; others rate it inferior. Truth to tell, it fits all categories, as there are three distinct parts to the normal song. It begins with the sound of a fiddle being tuned, which scraping is unmelodic whether the instrument is in the hands of a virtuoso or the freckle-faced kid down the street. Then comes a series of notes that ripple after the fashion of a house wren but which contain a glassy quality not to be found in the more familiar bird's effervescence. It ends on a weakly whistled note. All parts are on different pitches while the bird itself may be at different elevations, either trying to keep two reed stems from spreading farther apart, or fluttering down from a modest height. Raillike, marsh wrens are easily provoked into song. A sudden noise may start one, and he starts another, until the whole marsh is vibrating. When the night is still and sounds carry far, slamming doors and barking dogs nowhere near the marsh will produce a chorus that is far from a moonlight sonata.

Notwithstanding this wren's great liking for marshes, only certain ones will do. The marsh wren seems to be more common in coastal areas than inland, suggesting it evolved in the salt marsh and then spread inland along rivers with marshy edges. It seems to prefer marshes grown with narrow-leaved cattail, giving broad-leaf cattail a wide berth unless the latter has bulrushes and common reeds for companions. It does insist on extra-large areas, the better, perhaps, to keep you at a distance.

All wrens are perpetually fussy bodies, the marsh variety being no exception, fidgeting in the rank marsh growth as much as the house wren does around the woodpile. Having none of the phlegmatic qualities of, say, the black-billed cuckoo, wrens are not particularly faithful birds, the marsh wren least of all. Not that the male leaves a succession of deserted spouses; rather, his superabundance of energy allows him to keep a harem of sorts. His various mates of the moment will be neighbors, but still scattered over a reasonable area.

He is also an indefatigable house-builder. Arriving in the spring before the female he will initiate a frenzy of nest-building that persists well into the nesting season. None of these nests will be lined, nor would any be suitable for eggs or young as the whole construction lacks the skill and finesse of the female. Because of his unceasing energy, cock nests are fresher and greener than the one housing the young he has fathered. Speculation on the purpose of these dummy nests is rampant. He long ago forgot how to incubate and to brood, so perhaps he is on the way to leaving all household chores to his mate.

Like most other wrens, marsh wrens have a habit we deplore, one which, to their way of thinking, guarantees the sanctity of their nests and the safety of their young. Other species comparable in size are not allowed to nest in the immediate vicinity; but as the marsh wren is too small to drive off larger ones like red-winged blackbirds or American bitterns, the wrens suffer the presence of such a species until its eggs are laid. Then they remove the presumed threat by puncturing the eggs of the trespassers.

Not so many years ago the pundits who bestow "official" English names on our birds dropped the longstanding "long-billed" from this species and both the "short-billed" and "marsh" from the smaller wren of the wetlands. The latter is now simply called "sedge wren," a more appropriate name as it inhabits the border of a marsh, that part not permanently wet. And even more recently, they placed both birds in the same genus.

Nest: Globular, of marsh vegetation attached to living marsh growth, occasionally suspended from a shrub, and lined with fine grasses, tendrils, cattail down and feathers; 3 feet or less above water, the entrance being on the side and provided with a sill inclining inward to prevent the eggs from rolling out. It is almost waterproof and is sometimes plastered with mud. Eggs: 4-8 (4-6), pale, dark or dull brown dotted or spotted darker brown, the markings often wreathing the larger end, subelliptical to oval, smooth and rather glossy. Incubation: 13-14 days, by the female alone. Food: Insects.

Marsh Wren

G. LOW 83—

G. LOW 83 —

Common Yellowthroat
Geothlypis trichas

Breeds from near the limit of trees in Alaska and Canada south to Mexico. Winters from the southern U.S. south to Central America and the West Indies.

When I first met this little warbler it was known from Prince Rupert to Key West and from St. John's to San Diego as the "Maryland yellowthroat." Visions of magnolia blossoms, large plantations and mint juleps were conjured up at each meeting. Then, in close succession, the American Ornithologists' Union elected to give the name "northern yellowthroat" to all the many subspecies found on this continent; and I visited Maryland for the first time, receiving the final jolt when I found that that state was not overrun with the yellowthroats. The bird now goes by the name shown above.

While the AOU and Maryland let me down, the bird never has. My earliest bird books gave me more than adequate preparation for our first meeting, which saw me flat on my stomach under some weedy growth, nose to bill with an agitated pair, whose nest I never did find. The raccoonlike mask of the male, the wrenlike actions of both, and the characteristic, rhythmic song that attracted me to them in the first place, were the words of Neltje Blanchan and F. Schuyler Mathews clothed in flesh, blood and feathers.

The song, unmistakable and so unforgettable, is one of the few bird songs easily rendered in syllabic English, and demonstrates that the yellowthroat was involved in witchcraft long before Samantha wrinkled her delightful nose and executed her magical powers for the benefit of television audiences. The song is of three to five (rarely, two or six) phrases with, usually, the final one an abbreviation of the preceding. The most popular rendering, in the ears of various writers, is *witchity witchity witchity witch*. But you are free to follow other authors and spell the word as *which*; finalize it as *ety* or *ery*; or break the phrasing with commas or dashes. If your enunciation is as clear as the bird's, you will still be right on the button. Some writers make it *whatcha-see?* or *which is it?* and in doing so are quoting very well. But *which way sir?, rapity rapity rapity*, *what a pity*, and so forth, are little better than Chapman's *I beseech you*. I favor the *witchity* form as that's what I heard when lying prone so many years ago.

But the species does have a varied repertoire, reflected both geographically (almost like a dialect) and individually, as each bird seems capable of bewitching you in a number of ways. Sometimes he offers a condensed form, like *witchy*; sometimes a more lengthy opus, *wee-witchity*. Usually the accent is on the *witch* of disyllabic forms and on the third syllable of the longer one.

If your attraction has been his melody and you advance to obtain a better view of the musician, he will break off abruptly, leaving you to be met instead by a blank wall of underbrush, briers, cattails and the like. From this tangle will now come a volley of vigorous scolding that sounds like a repeated *tcheck*, given with a peculiar huskiness that is at once identifiable. It is wrenlike but even more so is a snarling, grating chatter that expresses even greater disapproval of your intrusion. By now your only hope of viewing him is to call him from his moist retreat by squeaking, to which he is quite responsive.

If the yellowthroat were completely addicted to water, my tummy would have become very wet many years ago. But while some take up residence in bushy, weedy fields and pastures and along roads bordered by strong thickets, the majority do spend the witching hour in the overgrown edges of marshes, swamps and watercourses. And, of course, it is in such situations that his mate will go about her housekeeping.

She, by the way, refuses to masquerade, preferring the open visage of Columbine. She looks like him otherwise, being olive above with neither wing-bars nor marked tail corners. Her habitat usually gives her away, but if you do catch her away from home you'll find that her throat and upper breast and also her under tail-coverts are distinctly yellow, the space in-between a dingy white. I was intrigued by one hen yellowthroat whose belly was so dark it was almost black, but I deduced an adventitious stain was the reason.

Hide her nest from humans as she may, the cowbird has little trouble finding it. A number of years ago it was determined that the yellowthroat ranked seventh in the species victimized by that avian parasite. More recently, studies in Ontario put it about twentieth. The female yellowthroat is not so resourceful as the female yellow warbler, but she has been known to build over the cowbird's egg as the enterprising warbler does, even to enclosing two eggs if her *bête noire* was persistent.

The female might not be so burdened if her mate contented himself with singing from well within their chosen retreat; but, no, he frequently sings indiscreetly from a long rush or weed-stalk, often hitching up the podium at the same time, making himself even more conspicuous. And when carried away by the excitement of the season, he will rise on fluttering wings and sing from the air. His flight song is as confused as the bobolink's, although he does contrive to insert a *witchity* into it somewhere.

The low nest site invites such unwanted diners as snakes, turtles and small mammals, while fallen nestlings, floundering in water, satisfy the hunger of large fish and bullfrogs.

On migration, the yellowthroat joins its fellow warblers and flies high enough to strike towers and similar obstructions; once, its characteristic jerky flight carried it to England.

Nest: A bulky cup of grass, leaves and bark strips lined with finer grass, tendrils and rootlets, well hidden on the ground in a grass tussock or similar vegetation, or within 3 feet of the ground in a shrub or bush. Eggs: 3-5 (4), white or creamy white, speckled and spotted browns, black and lilac chiefly about the larger end, subelliptical, smooth and slightly glossy. Incubation: 12 days, by the female alone, although the male assists with the young. Two-brooded. Food: Seeds (rarely), spiders and insects.

Sharp-tailed Sparrow
Ammodramus caudacutus

Breeds in western Canada from near the tree line south to the northern U.S., about James Bay, and on the Atlantic coast from the Gulf of St. Lawrence south to North Carolina. Winters on the Atlantic coast from New York to Florida and around the Gulf of Mexico.

Progress cannot be denied. Where once the way to view this shy, furtive bird was to drive it out of its habitat with a dog or noisy beaters, finesse claimed ascendancy. The new technique was to make squeaking or kissing sounds in a rude imitation of a young bird or one in distress; then, electronics retired that gambit. Now, the accepted way is to play a tape recording of the bird's song. Such practices are almost entirely necessary to bring sharp-tailed sparrows under surveillance; but for those who find the expense of tape recorders prohibitive, I suggest the following: Fill a cauldron with cold water. Over a fire which you can build beside a marsh suspected of harboring these birds, bring an old-style soldering iron to a ruddy glow. Immerse the iron in the cold water. If you remember to give the rim of the cauldron two weak taps with a stick before or after the dunking, you will have produced a passable imitation of the song of the sharp-tail. (This bird sometimes sings in flight, but I earnestly recommend not to carry the experiment that far!)

My phonetic rendering of the song is: *tuck tuck zreeeeee*, but I think Allan Cruickshank's *cut up cheese* is vastly superior to any interpretation published; and, most correctly, it produces the gasping, insectlike, wheezy trill. While the bird sings in flight in early spring, usually toward nightfall, the weak, unmusical effort is more often given as the bird grasps two swaying salt-marsh grass stems. Perhaps the bird has

elected for a short song because of the unstable support of its usual dais.

The few fortunate to observe this little marsh skulker are still further reduced because of the bird's restricted range: the salt marshes of the Atlantic coast from the Maritimes to North Carolina; a portion of the St. Lawrence River; the area about James Bay; and the sloughs and tules of the prairie region of Canada and North Dakota. Elsewhere one has to be watchful (in September, chiefly) for a migrant that comes up for air, as it were; once in its chosen habitat or a reasonable facsimile, the sharp-tail is mighty difficult to put up, preferring to run through grass stems with the celerity and appearance of a mouse. Flushed birds fly low and weakly, dropping into cover with a down-pointing tail. Sometimes bolder individuals will reach the top of an isolated bush, up periscope briefly, then return to the lush cover. There are, of course, exceptions. Once I found a people-watcher viewing me from within the top of a shrubby willow, while another eyed me from an open but quite low perch. Identification of the latter was ridiculously easy, for the buffy triangle that surrounds the gray ear-patch was even more conspicuous as it reflected the golden glow of a setting September sun. I would not have been surprised had it blinked on and off like a "vacancy" sign.

Too often, though, no matter the season or locality, sparrows such as the sharp-tailed go unidentified, for the subject of this sketch is a close companion of the seaside sparrow of the coastal marshes, Le Conte's sparrow of western grassy plots, and the savannah sparrow of both locations. All are confoundingly similar in appearance and habits. And none, not even this species, has a tail ending in a point. The savannah's is forked; the others' rounded, but in their case each individual feather is pointed, giving that appendage a bristly tip. In flight, the seaside sparrow appears dark grayish above, the others brownish.

One course is to carry a good field guide to your and the species' favorite marsh where, if you sit quietly, birds will appear from time to time. Sharp-tails move about less furtively after nesting, and even in that season are sometimes in full view, feeding on the muddy banks of streams or ditches draining a salt marsh. See one in flight and you will be impressed by its buzzy character, the rapid wing-beats producing little speed. Catch one on the ground and you will see a quick-change artist, first a small, big-headed, short-tailed sparrow which, with a flick of the tail, transmutes into a small, scurrying rodent that carries its head low. The procedure will be preceded by its short, sharp, low *tchep* of alarm.

Nest: A cup woven of dried grass and seaweed lined with finer grasses; on the ground in a tussock, tall grass or seaweed (tule in the west). Although fastened to grass stems, the bottom is rarely elevated but is usually flush with the ground. Eggs: 4-5, pale greenish-white or greenish-blue, speckled with browns, most heavily about the larger end, subelliptical to short elliptical, smooth and slightly glossy. Incubation: 11 days, by the female alone, the male taking no part in the nesting or care of the young. Food: Seeds of grass, weeds and wild rice; spiders and insects.

Sharp-tailed Sparrow

G. LOW 83

Swamp Sparrow
Melospiza georgiana

Breeds from near the tree line in Canada south to the central U.S. Winters throughout the U.S., except in the extreme north.

It was during a Christmas bird census of many years ago that my companion and I took a side excursion into a frozen marsh. According to the late Jim Baillie, my partner was one of the best in field identification. He was British born and still retained bits of his native dialect, which sometimes left a listener slightly confused. When a sparrow, alarmed at our approach, dived into cover, I obtained but a momentary view of it and was uncertain if it had been a song or swamp sparrow. Realizing that George had been in a more advantageous position, I turned to him for confirmation, asking, "song?" George shook his head and replied, "swamp," rhyming the word with "tramp." As I was the enumerator of our party, I spent an exasperating and perplexed minute or so studying my checking-card until George came to my rescue by pointing to this species.

A swamp sparrow is not an exceptional find in winter in the north, nor is it extraordinary to find one in a marsh at that season, as it is rarely far from water except when migrating. The brushy edges of marshes or a similar wetland with bushy growth, a woodland swamp, or where alders and willows thicket quiet waters, are its goals at the end of its northern migration. It may seek similar quarters in the south in winter but will also be found in brushy uplands or dry fields of broom sedge, with a supply of water not too far away. On migration it may drop down anywhere, but in fall may feed, alone or with other sparrows, in weedy fields and, so they say, in similarly grown gardens, a statement I question. Perhaps mine is not that weedy, but I note, regretfully, that the swamp sparrow is not one of the more than one hundred species that have visited mine. Doubtless one will visit it when the above is rolling off the presses.

Our thrushes are among our most accomplished musicians. Their ethereal, liquid melodies would have inspired early European composers had they been able to hear them. The swamp sparrow is no less accomplished, but in another way. What other bird can sing two notes

simultaneously, each on a different pitch and in different time? So states Aretas A. Saunders, who cautions, though, that if the listener is not properly located he will hear only one note or the other. The song, consisting of a single note, is rapidly reiterated and, perhaps, a slightly accelerated one on one pitch, which can be written *weet-weet-weet* almost ad infinitum. Many authors mistakenly call this a trill which, musically, must consist of two notes alternating about a tone apart. Some swamp sparrows do sing a two-note phrase that slurs upward, but this still cannot be defined as a trill. (This form seems to have been described by L. L. Snyder as *tootie-tootie-tootie*.) Moonlight sonatas are commonplace, as is also an autumnal chorus, while flight songs are occasional. The swamp sparrow is, in fact, as vocal as the rails that abide in the same marshy ground.

The commonly heard reiteration, which may, of course, be either the bass or the treble of the bird's two-handed effort, is like the simple songs of the chipping and field sparrows and the junco. In saccharinity it ranks between the songs of the field and the chippy, being sweeter, slower, more melodious and louder than the latter's.

The swamp sparrow's call note is not particularly distinctive, being a sharp, metallic *chink* a little too similar to the note of the white-throated sparrow for positive identification at times.

The song is sometimes the only indication of the bird's presence, as it is remarkably adept at keeping out of sight. Except when a male mounts a low perch to sing his unpretentious melody, swamp sparrows spend their time like so many mice, running or creeping about reedy stalks growing in a morass. They also emulate field voles in a dry field in winter. Sometimes you may catch one adroitly climbing stems of marsh plants or even walking over the flotsam and jetsam on shallow water; nor has it any hesitation in wading like a little sandpiper as it picks

insects and fallen seeds from the water's surface. The bird has been seen to pick at sun-dried dead fish, an act I am inclined to dismiss as curiosity rather than one stemming from hunger.

When flushed, it flies but a short distance, pumping its tail in the style of the song sparrow, from which, at such times, it is distinguished by its darker wings and tail. The wings also have some rust, lacking in the other bird. When the bird is at rest, the reddish cap and gray, unstreaked breast are good field marks. The less robust chipping sparrow has a reddish cap, too, but also has a black line right through the eye, not just back of it. Tree, field and white-throated sparrows all have more prominent wing-bars, while the white-throat's white throat is more expansive and conspicuous. The fine relationship of swamp, song and Lincoln's sparrows is reflected in the very close similarity of juvenile birds, the identification of which is best left to experts.

The male aids somewhat in nest-building but then drops out of the picture until the eggs hatch, although he has been known to feed a brooding mate. The rake, though, is inclined to polygamy and may be cohabiting with another mate while his first is engaged in house chores. Although the nest is frequently arched, the several I have seen, including two the year this was written, were quite open above. All were very difficult to relocate, while their original finding was quite fortuitous.

Nest: Cuplike, of grasses and sometimes leaves and rootlets; lined with finer grasses, hair or leaves, frequently arched, presenting a side entrance. Eggs: 4-5, variable in color, pale bluish-green to bluish-white, blotched, spotted and speckled reddish and other shades of brown and with light purple; subelliptical, smooth and slightly glossy. Incubation: 12-13 days, by the female alone. Two-brooded. Food: Seeds of grain, sedges, polygonums, vervain and ragweed; berries; insects.

Red-winged Blackbird

Agelaius phoeniceus

Breeds from near the tree line in Canada south to Central America and the West Indies. Winters throughout the U.S. except in the extreme north, in Central America and in the West Indies.

It is very easy to credit this bird of the marshes as being the catalyst to bird study. I strongly suspect it was so in my case, at a period so long ago it is but a blur of confusing memories. It is a natural conclusion, of course, as interest in birds is most prevalent in the spring, that glorious time of year when warm sunshine is redolent of an earthy smell and Dutchman's breeches sail in spanking fashion across the March sky; or when zephyrs of April, pungent with the odor of skunk cabbage and leek, caress trees fuzzy with the green down of arboreal adolescence. And all topped by one truly spring call, the fluting song of the red-wing.

I dimly recall one marshy pond where tail-spreading males sang in gesturing concert, each trying to outgurgle its fellows. That pond still exists, but the "conservation" measures practiced by the management of the park it borders have reduced the reed-bed to less than a garden plot, so that the operatic chorus has been dropped to, at best, a trio. The housing developments of encroaching civilization eliminated all but two of the eight attractive marshes in my beloved Humber Valley, another spot where early red-wings were welcomed before birds became objects of serious study.

Those scarlet-daubed blackbirds were of a single thought: To stake and hold a nesting territory for the females which would not appear for perhaps another three weeks. Territorial claims were laid by song, posturing, and display of the gaudy red and buff epaulets. Physical combat was sometimes threatened but never materialized, as a chased bird somehow always eluded its pursuer; or, perhaps, the following one, anxious to avoid fisticuffs, slowed down. When the females did arrive, the welkin would so resound with a cacophonous medley of liquid notes, all sounding as if blown or whistled through one of the reeds the birds lived by, and all with a background of constantly piped *peets* from the females, that one was glad, sometimes, to escape to the quiet roar of city traffic.

Any other of our native birds, dismayed by diminishing swamp, marsh and reedy, brushy growth about waterways, would have thrown in the sponge years ago. Not so the red-wing. Long will (not may!) his scarlet flag wave. As his wetlands fell to progress, he moved to meadows, even to those not permanently moist. In fact, the birds are now just as attuned to a good growth of grass as they are to a cattail marsh; and rather than squeeze their song from some swaying bulrush do so now from the solid foundation of a wood fence post.

This selection of drier fields facilitates things for the nest-seeking birder. I recall a chance meeting with a friend so inclined in the long ago. Barefoot, and with trousers rolled to his knees, he was cautiously treading the ooze of a heavily grown marsh, a jacket pocket sagging with the weight of beautifully scrawled eggs. Contrarily, I, dry shod, have merely crossed a grassy field at random, marking the spot from where each female rose, easily adding to my collection of nest photographs, as it is not my practice to take eggs or to disturb a nest unduly. On one occasion, having left my camera in my car, I made a mental note of the location of a nest — and have yet to rediscover the spot, although my subsequent search generated a chorus of angry *tsecks* and even a few nasal, petulant *teeabs*, the red-wing's alarm note.

Ornithologists have agreed on many things

concerning this bird, one of the most abundant North American species. One is that the song, almost invariably of three syllables, ends in a gurgly trill represented by a string of *eeee's*. Various interpretations have the first syllable beginning with a consonant (*c, k* or *qu*), and ending with *on, ong,* or *onk,* although some writers restrict this syllable to a single *o*. The second, and highest syllable is spelled *qua, ga, ka, la, sa* or *kla* with *e* substituting for *a* if desired. Then follows the prolonged *ree* or *lee,* which A. A. Saunders maintains is given on the third E above middle C, 90 per cent of the time. I lack instruments to check that in the field, but strong tonal sense suggests he is right. A few writers have heard the bird sing *gl-oogle-eee* or *gug-lug-geee*; while F. Schuyler Mathews had the bird in the tea business, selling *oo-long-tea* along with the improbable varieties, *you-choo-tea, shoo-chong-tea* and *quang-se-tea*. I have always heard it as *o-ka-lee,* perhaps because that is the first way I saw it written, although I quite agree that the red-wing *ke-conquereeeed* the marsh ages ago.

There is also agreement that the species does inestimable good in ridding us of insect pests and weed seeds, the first in summer, the latter in fall and early spring, when the birds are found in the fields in flocks of sometimes thousands. In autumn, such flocks have despoiled grain fields in the west and rice crops in the south. But the biggest complaint is of comparatively recent origin. In winter, joining grackles and starlings in numbers totaling millions to roost in some favored area, they become unmitigated nuisances. Drastic control measures have been required, some of which roused the ire of naturalists because of the indiscriminate killing.

How pleasant it would be if we could disperse such flocks with a device as simple as the red-wing's scarlet insignia. These red, buff-bordered feathers at the bend of the wing may be raised to eye-catching prominence when the male tries to impress a likely female. They are definitely used to intimidate others when staking territory and to warn other males away. I saw one bird, perched in a tree, flash angry red when another male made an innocent flight at considerable height above it. I have also seen such a display when a bird wished to preempt my feeding station, although starlings and various sparrows were the only other birds around at the time. Still another display was given a cowbird that ventured too close while both foraged under the feeder. Even I, sitting in my own garden hopefully awaiting the reappearance of a rare warbler, was warned away from the sunflower-seed feeder by a preemptive male!

Young males dress in drag or close to it, so that, in fall, there is a variety of costumes. Once I saw one with a white wing-patch identical to that of the yellow-headed blackbird; and I have also seen, near Toronto, one heavily streaked and with the almost solid black body of the tricolored blackbird of coastal California.

Nest: A deep, woven cup of grasses, reeds, weeds and rootlets lined with finer materials; sometimes in a grass tussock on the ground or in a bush or tree overhanging water, but usually tied to marsh vegetation 4 inches to 12 feet up. Eggs: 3-5 (4), pale bluish-green or bluish-white, variously marked with shades of black, purple, brown or gray, subelliptical to long elliptical, smooth and glossy. Incubation: 11-12 days, by the female alone, the male assisting with the care of the young. Food: Seeds of grass, grain, wild rice, smartweed, ragweed; fruit; snails, worms, spiders, crustaceans and insects.

Red-winged Blackbird

Yellow-headed Blackbird

Xanthocephalus xanthocephalus

Breeds from central British Columbia and the Canadian prairies south to the southern U.S. Winters in southwestern U.S. and Mexico.

Every time I ventured west of the Great Lakes, which was not often in the earlier years of my birding, I breathed a fervent prayer that I be allowed to behold this strikingly marked dweller of the tules and cattails. But because the bird is rare and local in those few places I did visit then, my entreaties were never answered. Came a fall day and my wife and I were jouncing over a short road badly rutted by traffic in the wet weather preceding, our objective being the rim of a precipice overlooking the large bay of Hamilton, Ontario and its contingent of ducks. Driving slowly and cautiously, eyes riveted to the longitudinal washboard beneath us, my peripheral vision picked up bird life on our right. One bird, I felt sure, was a flicker. Just as I prepared to brake at the end of our course, my sigh of relief was changed to a gasp when my wife asked, incredulously, "A blackbird with a yellow head?" I looked to the right, naturally, as it had been there I had seen bird movement, and saw only the flicker bounding away. My wife then informed me that the vagrant to southern Ontario had been on our left and was now out of sight.

Many years later, looking down on a large pond or small lake nestling in one of British Columbia's many valleys, I wondered if my unseen bird were one of the animated dandelions I could see walking about the muddy shores.

Those particular yellow-heads, and the Hamilton visitor, were out of place; for while they resort to nearby open lands to feed during the nesting season, the home marsh of those birds was nowhere to be seen. And, unlike the red-wing, the yellow-head insists on a marsh for nesting — a marsh, if you please, with its emergent vegetation standing in from three to ten feet of water; or, if high and dry, surrounded by a moat.

The red-wing and his mate will abide as a solitary pair, although they do find much more fun in a crowd. The yellow-head, on the other hand, is far from a loner. Nesting has no privacy, although to be sure, the nests do not come close to touching. Nor do the young spend much time with only siblings for playmates, for as soon as they are fit, the mob heads for grain fields, sometimes raising the ire of farmers. Later in the season they noisily converge on stubble fields, while visits to corrals, barnyards and pastures are made at any time. As the seasons change, the flocks increase in size, mingling with red-wings, grackles, cowbirds and Brewer's blackbirds, all to retire to the marsh for a night's sleep preceded by much squabbling. Clannish as is the species, and its numbers in a marsh roost after nesting may approach a half-million birds, there is a strange sexual discrimination evident in their selection of winter quarters, the males, in the adult form at least, wintering apart.

Numerous as is the species at times, it does not attract the same attention as some others of their kin; it is their custom on arrival in spring to go directly to their selected marsh. This, because of its usual inaccessibility, is infrequently visited by humans. Safe within, the birds continue to escape notice.

This is a pity really, as the posturing accompanying a male's "song" must be seen in order to ignore his inability as a musician. His three opening notes do show promise but quickly deteriorate into a harsh jumble during which he seems to suffer a choking spell that concludes in a prolonged, descending, rasping buzz. An unoiled hinge is a symphonic measure in comparison. In life, though, he starts out well, musically speaking, as young males have a heavy, rolling call nowhere near as harsh or ridiculous as the effort of their male parents. But the adolescents proceed to shoot the budget on clothes rather than on music lessons. The adult male is, of course, in proper company; except for the orioles and a few others, the family of icterids, especially those that are largely black, are long on effort, short on melody.

As he associates with red-wings so readily, it is well to note the differences in flight. Both follow an undulating course in a somewhat slow, deliberate manner; but a flock of yellow-heads will be strung out loosely, featuring length; the more compact red-wing flock will be wide rather than long. Incidentally, the yellow-head and the two kinds of red-wings he associates with will drive any hawk from their premises.

It is during courtship that he stands, or rather, flies supreme among the blackbirds. He begins by flying toward a female with both his head and feet lowered and his wings held in such a way as to display his white wing-patches. This invariably makes no impression on her. There may follow an aerial chase ending with grotesque posturing on the ground.

The common grackle swaggers when on the ground, and so does the yellow-head — but with a pomposity lacking in the other. It was that characteristic that helped me identify one in British Columbia. The bird, without a single black feather, flew into the alkaline margin of a slough, marking the fourth full albino I had ever seen. Helping in the identification was a slight lemon tint on the head and neck. Fully described, the bird was an amalgam of color, truly an all-white, yellow-headed blackbird. Perhaps it was one of my animated dandelions gone to seed.

Nest: A woven basketlike cup of marsh vegetation lined with finer grasses; attached to reeds and cattails from one to 3 feet above water up to 10 feet deep. Eggs: 3-5 (4), green, gray or dull grayish-white, heavily speckled and blotched browns and grays, long subelliptical to long oval, smooth and glossy. Incubation: 12-13 days, by the female alone. Food: Seeds of grain (mostly waste) and weeds; insects, their eggs and larvae.

The Jackdaws

Great-tailed Grackle
Cassidix mexicanus

Boat-tailed Grackle
Cassidix major

Great-tailed: Breeds and winters in Arizona, New Mexico, Texas and adjacent Mexico. Boat-tailed: Breeds on the Atlantic coast from New Jersey south to Florida and around the Gulf to Galveston, Texas.

The title of this sketch is the name commonly given to two species whose "book" names may be confusing, as they seem to have been interchangeable in the past. Indeed, were this book to be in Spanish, separate names would be used for the male and female of each species.

There had long been a growing suspicion that the very long-tailed grackles that waddle and swagger about parts of the southern United States were two separate species. So in 1973, contrary to the prevailing policy, the American Ornithologists' Union split rather than lumped two forms. The two subspecies, *Cassidix mexicanus major* and *C. m. torreyi* were removed from the *mexicanus* group and elevated to specific status, with the names *C. major major* and *C. m. torreyi*, respectively. As is usual in such scientific moves, the reason seems a little obscure. Most moves of that kind seem nothing more than hair-splitting, although perhaps "feather-splitting" is a more appropriate phrase.

The species *C. major*, which confounds its scientific name as it is the smaller one, is found along coastal United States from New Jersey to the tip of Florida and around the Gulf of Mexico to Galveston, Texas. It is the salt-water bird except in Florida, where it is found in and about inland marshes and fresh-water ponds and lakes. The larger species, *C. mexicanus*, takes up where the other leaves off in Texas and continues down the coast into South America. This form, though, not only follows the Rio Grande into New Mexico, but readily accepts the arid conditions away from that river, nesting in mesquite, chaparral, cactus and yucca; the other species

invariably chooses a location conditioned by the salt-laden air from the nearby sea. Nevertheless, *mexicanus* does not seem to venture into the Sonoran desert itself but, from my experience, keeps to the cities and towns themselves, cities which, like Tucson, have gardens little different in plant life from the surrounding desert.

Other than size, the only difference in the two species seems to be in nesting and eating habits imposed by habitat conditions. There is, however, one incontestable fact. There is none of the interbreeding that clouds the specific distinction of birds like the rose-breasted and black-headed grosbeaks, the eastern and western bluebirds, the blue-winged and cinnamon teals and other obviously distinct forms.

Boat-tailed or great-tailed is, in the male plumage, nothing more than a superlarge common grackle, with the same strut, same swagger, same domineering personality, same taste for eggs and unfledged young and same liking for human habitations, although the boat-tailed does prefer a room with an ocean view. The female plumage is something else. While she has all the traits, likes and dislikes of her brassy-eyed mate, whom she may share — but only if her sex is the more numerous — she has as much finery as a female house sparrow. If the identity of a flock of grackles escapes you but if the flock contains long-tailed brownish individuals considerably smaller than the glossy ones, you will have in view a flock of one of the jackdaws. Female common grackles, on the other hand, are slightly smaller, duller replicas of their lords and masters. Unfortunately, this guide is valueless from the onset of incubation through the adolescence of the young, as the adult males form a carefree club and wander freely (and sometimes destructively) about the countryside, as do the combined sexes after nesting.

The indifference is far removed from the

Yellow-headed Blackbird

G. LOW 83 —

posturing and swaggering of a few weeks earlier, when the males, never tiring of exhibiting their iridescent plumage, posed and postured in the most ludicrous attitudes. Often in company with others of their kind, although not necessarily sex (and, Narcissus-like, sometimes when the only individual in a tree), all birds in the group will stop their movement to point bill to the zenith and remain in that position for an appreciable length of time, a trick borrowed from or lent to our brown-headed cowbird. The latter, though, plays statue only in spring; jackdaws apparently whenever in the mood.

Another characteristic of the males, very noticeable in flight, is the keeling of the long tail, where the outer feathers are curved upward so that the appendage resembles a long, glossy black trough. This keeling is not restricted to the jackdaws, but is also exhibited by the common grackle. In the latter, though, the exhibition is most evident and almost entirely in the spring, suggesting it has some sort of sexual motivation. I once advanced the theory that the keeling was to help the bird in the strong March winds of the north, but now remove my tongue from cheek and withdraw the supposition as preposterous. Jackdaws do keel during a greater part of the year, perhaps because their breeding season is protracted. In St. Lucia, I found Carib grackles keeling in August, but presume this was because those birds are never far removed from any nesting season.

Jackdaws may regard their tail with justifiable vanity, as it is inordinately lengthy and, especially in the southern species, widely splayed or graduated at the tip. Its length creates problems during strong winds which, catching the tail, will turn a grounded bird end to end and even head over tarsi. Their difficulties during tropical hurricanes must be immense.

All grackles are opportunists, the great-tailed being the most extreme. Anything edible, plant or animal, is relished. The birds' manner of foraging is just as varied, ranging from a painstaking search for grubs in newly plowed soil to digging for fiddler crabs in sand; from the removal of young birds by stealth to the open attack on freshly planted or ripening corn. Terrestrial approach is sometimes abandoned, as South American birds will swoop low over water to snare fish, while the less timorous will even dive like a tern or kingfisher. And, north or south, wading in shallows up to the breast is commonplace.

The vocal accomplishments of the jackdaws seem without end, except, of course, the shades of Bach and Beethoven must quaver at each rendition. A rolling call that seems to be common to all races of both species has been the subject of much debate, but I think the consensus is that it is partly vocal, partly mechanical, as the mandibles seem to snap when the sound is forthcoming. The South American race that ventures into the extreme parts of the United States has a prolonged, rising note, part squeal, part whistle. Once we dispense with those two specialties, we are obliged to listen to the same sort of discordant squeaks and squeals that are emitted by the common grackle of the north.

For those despairing of seeing these entertaining giants of grackleworld, take heart. The species *mexicanus* has been increasing its range north of the Mexican border, while *major*, which reached New Jersey in 1950, is becoming ever more common along the Atlantic coast.

Nest: In colonies; a bulky cup of grass, sticks, seaweed and Spanish moss lined with grass and rootlets with an additional lining of mud or dung; in bushes, trees or reeds, as much as 50 feet up. Eggs: 3-5 (3-4), pale blue or pale bluish-white, scrawled, spotted and blotched blackish and purplish, subelliptical to long oval, smooth and glossy. Incubation: 13-14 days, the male taking no part in nesting duties except to defend the breeding territory from predators. Food: Virtually omnivorous. Grains, berries, mollusks, crustaceans, insects, small fishes and young birds and eggs.

Great-tailed Grackle

Bibliography

Areas of Importance for Migratory Bird Protection in Ontario. Toronto: Ministry of Natural Resources.

Beardslee, Clark S., and Harold D. Mitchell. *Birds of the Niagara Frontier Region.* Buffalo: Buffalo Society of Natural Science (Bulletin 22). 1965.

Bent, Arthur Cleveland. *Life Histories of North American Marsh Birds.* New York: Dover, 1963.

_____. *Life Histories of North American Shore Birds.* Part II. New York: Dover, 1962.

_____. *Life Histories of North American Wild Fowl.* Vol. I. New York: Dover, 1951.

Blanchan, Neltje. *Birds Worth Knowing.* Garden City: Doubleday, Page, 1925.

Bond, James. *Birds of the West Indies.* London: Collins, 1971.

Chapman, Frank M. *The Warblers of America.* New York: Dover, 1968.

Cleugh, T., and P. Woodland, eds. *Fraser River Estuary Study; Habitat.* Victoria: Province of British Columbia, 1978.

Cowardin, Lewis M., Virginia Carter, Francis C. Golet and Edward T. LaRoe. *Classification of Wetlands and Deep-water Habitats of the United States.* Washington: Fish and Wildlife Services, U.S. Department of Interior, 1979.

Cruickshank, Allan D. *The Pocket Guide to Birds.* New York: Pocket Books, 1954.

Errington, Paul L. *Of Man and Marshes.* Ames: Iowa State University Press, 1957.

Harrison, Colin. *A Field Guide to the Nests, Eggs and Nestlings of North American Birds.* London: Collins, 1978.

Horwitz, Eilinor Lander. *Our Nation's Wetlands.* Washington: Council on Environment Quality, 1978.

Leopold, Aldo. *A Sand County Almanac.* New York: Oxford University Press, 1966.

Mansell, William, and Gary Low. *North American Birds of Prey.* Toronto: Gage, 1980.

Mathews, F. Schuyler. *Field Book of Wild Birds and their Music.* New York: Putnam's, 1921.

Niering, William A. *The Life of the Marsh.* New York: McGraw-Hill, 1966.

Palmer, Ralph S. *The Shorebirds of North America.* (Gardner D. Stout, ed.) New York: Viking, 1967.

Peterson, Roger Tory. *A Field Guide to the Birds.* Boston: Houghton Mifflin, 1939.

Ripley, S. Dillon. *Rails of the World.* Toronto: M. F. Feheley, 1977.

Saunders, Aretas A. *A Guide to Bird Song.* New York: Appleton-Century, 1935.

Simmons, G. E., chairman. *Fraser River Estuary Study; Summary.* Victoria: Province of British Columbia, 1978.

Snyder, L. L. *Ontario Birds.* Toronto: Clarke, Irwin, 1951.

Vesey-Fitzgerald, Brian. *A Book of British Waders.* London: Collins, 1939.

Index

Design
Marg. Round

Typesetting
Canadian Composition Limited

Typeface
Garamond

Color Separations
Colourgraph Reproduction Inc.

Printing
McLaren Morris and Todd Limited

Paper
Sterling Matte

Binding
John Deyell Company